Tommy Tedesco
FOR GUITAR PLAYER

Alfred Publishing Co., Inc.
16320 Roscoe Blvd., Suite 100
P.O. Box 10003
Van Nuys, CA 91410-0003
alfred.com

ISBN-10: 0-7390-5381-7
ISBN-13: 978-0-7390-5381-2

A Tribute from the Los Angeles Guitar Players

In my career as a guitarist, I have seen many methods for the guitar covering a variety of subjects. In my travels as a guitarist, I have probably been asked one question more than others: "What does a studio guitarist need to know?"

This book answers that question more completely than any other I have ever seen. It also covers a variety of subjects that have never been touched on before and, until now, could only be learned through years of experience.

I have had the pleasure of sitting next to Tommy Tedesco on studio dates, and in my estimation, Tommy Tedesco is one of the best, if not the best studio guitarist in the world.

Aside from the musical information, there is a wealth of human interest to be found in this book. You could call it a bible for guitar players. I will have to buy one and so should you.

—Joe Pass

Most people agree that Los Angeles is the recording capitol of the world. If you are the number-one guitarist in the L.A. studios as long as Tommy has been, you can consider yourself a great guitarist and musician. Tommy Tedesco is not only one of the great guitarists in Los Angeles, he is one of the great guitarists in the world.

When I first played with Tommy Tedesco, I was maybe 21. It was a TV movie. When I arrived at the session, being young and experienced, and (as Tommy puts it) "slightly cocky," I sat down in front of the 1st guitar book. When Tommy arrived and saw what I did, he didn't get upset or "bad vibe" me for the rest of the day, he just merely switched the guitar books and with his pencil scratched out "Guitar II" on the music cover and wrote "Guitar I" for me. That lesson taught me a lot that day and every time I work with Tommy, he teaches me more. Study this book carefully because Tommy "knows." He can offer you some incredible information.

P.S. Thanks for all your help, Tommy.

—Lee Ritenour

There are few, if any, guitarist who have such outstanding capabilities in so many musical areas as Tommy Tedesco. His technical command of the instrument most certainly borders on perfection. What makes his technique important is he has a great gift of interpretation and melodic feel.

As a studio guitarist, Tommy would have to be the best I have ever played with. I am pleased that Tommy is sharing some of his musical knowledge with us. We will all be better off for it.

—Herb Ellis

The information that Tommy Tedesco is offering in this book is priceless—a must for every guitar player. He is definitely one of a kind with as much experience to draw on as any person I know.

Take advantage of this. Tommy is genius, gentlemen—the epitome of what a studio player should be.

—Larry Carlton

DEDICATION

I dedicate this book to the guitar world. Guitar players, some of them friends, some I've never met, some that are no longer with us but all had a part in my developing a love for the guitar (in alphabetical order).

Laurindo Almeida   Al Hendrickson
Bob Bain   Barney Kessel
Dennis Budimir   Pat Martino
Vince Brundo   Lou Morell
Charlie Christian   Joe Pass
Pete Cicero   Jimmy Rainey
Herb Ellis   Howard Roberts
Tal Farlow   Johnny Smith

Also to the memory of my father, Henry N. Tedesco, who found the way to scrape together $1.00 every week for my guitar lessons during the 1930's. And to my mother, Rose, who would keep my father off my back when I didn't practice.

And to my wife, Carmeline, and my children, Dale, Denny, Desiree, and Damon, who have put up with my craziness all my life.

TOMMY TEDESCO'S CREDITS

RECORDINGS BY:

Roger Williams
Shelley Manne
Vicki Carr
Barbara Streisand
Rod McKuen
Martin Denny
Benny Goodman
Chet Baker
Tijuana Brass
Jan and Dean
Beach Boys
Ventures
Ray Charles
Roberta Flack
Henry Mancini
Les Brown
Sarah Vaughn
Carmen McRae
Simon & Garfunkle
5th Dimension
Steve Bishop
Kenny Loggins
Phil Spector
Frank Sinatra
Tony Bennett
Glen Campbell
Perry Como
Joan Baez
Jimmy Rogers
Claudine Longet
Andy Williams
Doris Day
Burl Ives
Peggy Lee
Diana Ross
Anita Kerr
Johnny Mann
Michele LeGrande
John Williams
Hugo Montenegro
Percy Faith
Baja Marimba
Four Freshman
Lettermen
Sandpipers
Tiny Tim
Partridge Family
Sammy Davis, Jr.

TV SERIES AND SPECIALS:

Starsky & Hutch
Kojak
Operation Petticoat
Love Boat
Carol Burnett
Mickey Mouse Club
Switch
Happy Days
Laverne & Shirley
M*A*S*H*
Three's Company
Mary Tyler Moore
Police Woman
Family
Baa Baa Black Sheep
Love American Style
Waltons
Barnaby Jones
Medical Center
Colombo
Baretta
Bionic Woman
Rockford Files
Quincy
Academy Awards
Emmy Awards
Critics Awards
Grammy Awards
Sinatra Specials
Charlie's Angels
Switch
Six Million Dollar Man
Police Story
Fernwood Tonight
Gong Show
Soap
Alice
Rhoda
Bob Newhart
Lou Grant
Roots
Holocaust
Wonder Woman
Eight Is Enough
How the West Was Won

MOVIES:

Airport
Bonnie & Clyde
Butch Cassidy & The Sundance Kid
Enter the Dragon
Freebie and the Bean
Poisidon Adventure
Silent Movie
Young Frankenstein
Conrack
Cool Hand Luke
French Connection
Love Story
All the President's Men
The Godfather
Towering Inferno
Deer Hunter
California Suite
Boulevard Nights

TOMMY'S ALBUMS:

The Guitars of Tom Tedesco
— United Artists

Twangy Twelve Great Hits
— DOT

Twelve String Guitar
— United Artists

Calipso Beat
— United Artists

Tommy Tedesco - When Do We Start
— Discovery Records

Tommy Tedesco - Autumn
— Discovery Records

Tommy Tedesco - Alone at Last
— Discovery Records

FOREWORD

I first heard about Tommy Tedesco in the early 60's. All the musicians I talked to that had worked with him spoke in glowing terms about his playing. When I finally got to work with him I expected another "hot shot" rock and roll guitar player but I was wrong. He astounded me with his all around ability, classical, R & R, flamenco, and jazz. He handled all music as if it were the only music he played. The opportunity for real jazz playing was practically nil in the studios at this time. But in between tunes he would fool around playing jazz with the rhythm section. I could tell right away that his was a talent that should be given a chance to be heard by more people. I kept after Tommy to come out of the studios and be seen and heard in the jazz settings in night clubs. I finally talked him into playing on a Cole Porter Jazz album I was doing. He had such a ball and played so well he hasn't stopped doing it since. Results can be heard on his albums "*When Do We Start*" and "*Autumn*". Both have been released on Discovery-Trend Records.

Tommy is a legendary figure in Studio guitar playing. He is probably one of the most recorded players in the history of the music business. After working with various jazz groups in the western New York area, Tommy left to go on the road with the Ralph Marterie Orchestra. This was in 1953. When the Marterie Orchestra played the Hollywood Palladium in Hollywood, Tommy loved the West coast and decided to settle down there. He returned to Niagara Falls, New York (his home town) to pick up his wife and child and left for the West coast.

The first couple of years were a struggle for the Tedesco's. He worked in the warehouse of the Douglas Aircraft to enable him to support his family. All of his off time was spent practicing guitar. The day he quit his day job and played his guitar for a living was the happiest day of his life.

When the 1960's arrived Tommy could be found running from studio to studio doing a variety of studio work, records, TV, movies, TV and radio commercials. His versatility really showed thru in these times. He could be heard on pop dates such as the Beach Boys, Jan and Dean, Tijuana Brass, Bobby Darin, Wayne Newton, Vicki Carr, 5th Dimensions, Diana Ross and the Supremes, etc. In the same week he could be found doing Jazz dates for performers such as Sarah Vaughn, Carmen McRae, Peggy Lee, Bud Shank, and Chet Baker, and etc. In these early years there was hardly a popular singer that recorded on the West Coast that didn't have Tommy's guitar work on their record at one time or another.

When the 1970's rolled around, Tommy settled into doing mostly movie and TV shows. When a part was considered to be difficult and demanding, Tommy's name was at the top of the leader's list.

In 1976 Tommy collaborated with *Guitar Player Magazine* to do a steady article on Studio guitar playing. This was Tommy's initiation to education of the guitar player. His interest in this new field was expanded when he started to do monthly clinics for the Guitar Institute of Technology in Hollywood on Studio guitar playing.

Tommy considers the guitar a lifetime of love and learning of which neither ever stops.

Shelly Manne

AUTHOR'S COMMENTS

I have geared this book for three (3) types of guitar players.

GUITAR PLAYER (1)

This type of guitar player is a devoted student of the instrument. He will absorb the material, work hard and after a few years will be on his way to being a successful player.

GUITAR PLAYER (2)

He is a little lazy. He will pick up a few things from this book and keep the book until he feels he has the time and energy for playing the guitar. When the calling hits him, he is just as dedicated as guitar player (1). He also stands a good chance of being a player. (As a youth I fell into this category.) I hated to practice. My teacher, John Morell, back in Niagara Falls, New York, till this day cannot understand me playing a guitar for a living. He said of the thousands of students he taught, I was the worst. (I remember he was right.) I was in my early 20's when the calling for the guitar hit. For the next few years, I practiced and played for hours at a time and saw giant results. It is never too late if you have the determination and the patience to work at it.

GUITAR PLAYER (3)

This player owns a guitar. He keeps waiting for someone to touch his shoulder with a magic wand and overnight he is a great player. This won't happen. A guitar player is not made without a lot of work. For this player I have included a few tips on life that can be used even by non-guitar players. He can read the book and see some different slants on the business. But forget him as a player. It will never happen.

In this book I have written things that helped me through the years. I have included exercises to develop picking techniques. Also I have tried to show the approach in sight reading I have used. (Position type reading, Exercises on different string combinations, Low and high note reading, Chord form reading, Syncopation, Other time signatures, Combining time signatures, Chord symbol reading, and Vertical chord reading, etc.)

In the studio section of the book, I have tried to describe studio work in five different studio categories (Records, Live television, Commercials, Television films, and Movies.)

In the latter part of the book, I have a section called LIFE SAVING DEVICES. In this section I show examples of tricks I have used to get the part done with a minimum of effort. Little hints for a player that could be invaluable for years to come are also included in this section.

I received tremendous help in writing this book from Jon Kurnick, a young guitarist that works in my quartet. Even though Jon is in his early 20's, he has the knowledge of a musician that has studied for 40 years. Jon studied music at the University of Santa Barbara. He has a well rounded background in his work. Jon has played jobs of all styles. (Country Western, Rock and Roll, Classical, Jazz, and has worked with many singers.) He is the most talented young guitar player I have met in many years. Without his help it would have been an almost impossible task to complete this book because of my work schedule.

As far as I am concerned about the book, it can be worth from nothing to thousands of dollars earned to a player. One little thing learned can possibly create a job for you. So many of these things I have told professional guitarists around me. They have come back to thank me for it. I hope guitar players in categories 1 and 2 really find a lot of helpful advise. As far as guitar players in category 3, I will ask you if we ever meet face to face if you enjoyed the little tips and stories I have included in the book.

Sincerely yours,

Tommy

TABLE OF CONTENTS

LIFE SAVING DEVICES FOR THE STUDENT

I have never met a guitar player that didn't think he had the best guitar in the world. (At least until he buys his next one.) So here's what to do with your best guitar: blow a few weeks in a room, find what strings are the best for your sound, what action on the guitar makes you sound the best. Know your guitar in and out. After this, do the same with your amplifier and other equipment. Experiment . . .

When you sit in with a group, use only your own equipment. This gives them "your" sound. Don't let strange equipment be the reason you don't get the job. The complete sellable product is your sound, don't blow it.

If you can't play perfectly in tune, buy one of the tuners that are on the market. It will save you much aggravation for years to come. One Los Angeles player lost thousands of dollars because he had an intonation problem.

Try to go to an occasional pop concert even though you might not like the music. Spend time watching the conductor. This will end up being an extremely valuable experience.

Listen to all kinds of guitar players. Know their names and the style they are known for. This helps when a leader asks for a specific style of guitar playing.

Don't nickel and dime yourself in terms of money. Sometimes you won't get paid enough at the start. Don't complain, your day will come. Don't let a few dollars be in the way of the leader calling you for future work.

When you are taking a break from practicing and and are relaxing watching TV, play your guitar softly. Work on techniques. Your eyes and ears will be watching TV but your hands will be busy building techniques in your off time.

Don't rush out and buy expensive equipment until you can really afford and warrant it. The guitar won't make you a player. If I rushed out and bought Arnold Palmer golf clubs, I will still be a hacker with good golf clubs.

I haven't known a giant on guitar that didn't live, eat, and sleep guitar. If this is not you, don't panic . . . You probably won't be in a guitar players' Hall of Fame, but you will lead a good comfortable life playing the instrument of your choice.

Change strings when they go dead or bad in tuning. Not just because a week or a month is up. I have had the same strings on my 6 string bass guitar for 15 years. (Not advice, just fact.)

Take all kinds of jobs for experience such as jazz, rock, latin, society, shows, country and western, dixie, etc. It's amazing what you can learn about a certain style after working in a club with that style. I took a country and western job for two weeks many years ago and I learned more in those two weeks about country playing than I had in the previous ten years.

When you take a job, it should have one or more of these qualities:

1. Good money
2. Fun
3. Connections for the future
4. Learning

If it doesn't have any of these, forget it. Move on.

Whenever I had a pitfall in my career, I would rush home and practice. After many pitfalls, it forced me into being a better player. Don't practice what comes easy. Practice what is giving you a difficult time.

Learn from each other. I have picked up things from other guitar players that were novices. Don't be jealous of each other. Share your experiences and licks and you will both be farther ahead.

As a youth, form your own band. No matter how bad it is, it will get better. Start playing jobs as early as possible. Money - no object. Learn, learn, learn . . .

A player looking at studio parts sometimes says, "I could play that part." He doesn't realize the guitar player that is there is generally there for what he has done in the past. Or what he can do is needed. Don't let the simple parts fool you. There are plenty of times a player has to pull out all of his tricks to play a part.

Sit in with strange groups when you get a chance. It provides more outlets to getting future work.

Every once in a while take a challenging job that might be a little above where you are. If it comes off, it's good for the head trip.

Do not put down anyone around you in the music business, even the non-musician. Recording engineers, music copyists, set up men, etc., can have a hand in helping or hurting your career. I have gotten plenty of jobs because these non-musician people have verified my work to composers.

Meet the guitar players. This is more than likely where your start will come from. Don't be overbearing and too cocky. Let your playing be your selling point. Sooner or later if you are a player, help will come your way.

When you see a part for the first time, check out all repeats and signs. If you neglect this, you will find yourself lost in the part that should have been relatively easy.

If you are practicing reading and get tired, stop and rest. You will get nothing out of practicing while being fatigued.

If you feel you are a "player" and live in a town that is limited musically, leave! Go to the big town. Besides this offering more opportunity, you will be amazed at the learning process, just being near great players, does for your playing.

We all think we are going nowhere in our playing. Look back a year. You will probably realize you have come a long way. Have your yearly checkup. If you haven't improved, time to soup up your practicing and playing skills.

As a check to see if you are reading the notes on the music and not just memorizing a part, read the part backwards. This is a good check for a beginning reader.

If you have talent for the guitar and get discouraged, don't give up. Sooner or later it will come your way.

Many times when you are playing, panic might set in. You will feel your knees shaking and your hands trembling. Don't be discouraged. It can happen to anyone. Experience will lessen the fears.

Read all the written material that is on the part besides notes. For instance: take DS 2nd time, lay out first time, change to acoustic from electric, softer, louder, etc. Many times I work with young players that are good readers and I kid them, "You can read the notes but you are having a hard time reading English."

When someone helps you in your career, make a special call to thank them. It's the least you can do for their efforts.

Don't make fun of any style. Nobody wants to be criticized for what they do well, regardless of style. Keep your mouth shut about players.

As you move up the ladder, don't step all over the older players (or we'll get you).

x

PICKING
TECHNIQUES

XII

THE PICK (FLAT PICK)

HOLDING THE PICK:

I use the same technique in holding the pick as golfers do holding a golf club. Extend the right hand like you were going to shake hands. Close the hand. Put your pick between the thumb and first joint of the first finger. Bring your hand back to the guitar. You are ready to play. You will notice the pick is facing up towards the string not perfectly at a 45° angle. This enables a player to play much faster. As an alternate choice, extend the last three fingers out, having them touch the strings or the pick guard. This acts as an anchor for your hands. Do not anchor the wrist to the bridge to enable the hands to be free to pick near bridge or neck for different tonal variations. My wrist is very loose when I play.

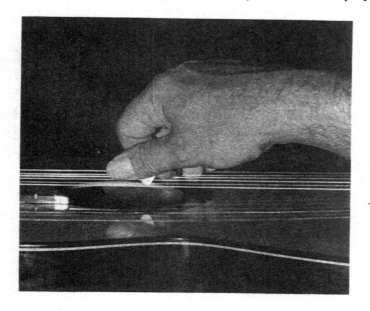

Note — You will notice that very little of the pick is extended outside the fingers.

USING A PICK FOR SOUND:

Try different picks for tone quality. Each different pick thickness gets a different sound. Many times I am asked to get a soft sound on the Classical guitar. I go to a heavier thick pick. This creates a sweet and mellow sound. The thinner picks bend, creating a slapping sound along with the string tone (remember playing cards in the bicycle spokes?).

SUPER PROFESSIONAL ADVICE:

If you are happy with your pick hand, don't change a thing. This method is for the student who is having a problem with picking. I've heard numerous guitar players with a lot of technique that all have a different system. Years ago there was a guitar player in Los Angeles, Milt Norman, that held the pick between his thumb and second finger. His technique was the fastest I ever heard at that time.

🎸 🎸 🎸 🎸 🎸 🎸 🎸 🎸 🎸 🎸 🎸 🎸 🎸 🎸 🎸 🎸 🎸

On a date I was doing a Jingle for Bob Thompson; at the beginning of the session I went to Bob and told him I would flip for the payment of the jingle. If I won I would get double scale. And if I lost I would donate my services. He accepted. We flipped. I lost . . . We ended up working for four (4) hours. I lost over $200.00 plus about $600.00 in reuses. "Stupid Gambler."

1

ALTERNATE PICKING

Alternate picking (down and up-up and down) is the most popular form of picking I use in my playing. This takes all the guess work out of my mind and I can concentrate on the notes.

UP-DOWN PICKING EXERCISES

These exercises should be played slowly at first. When you feel comfortable with the notes of the exercise, pick up speed.

The above exercise is great for the fourth finger. Repeat measure transposing up a ½ step each time until your hands cannot make it any more — rest! — Start over again.

The above exercise is great for crossing strings.

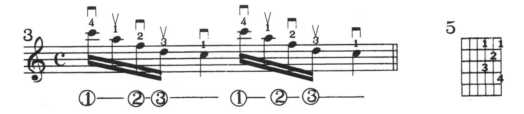

The above exercise is tougher than #2 because you descend down the neck. Upon completion of exercises 2 and 3, join them together and practice.

This exercise synchronizes the left hand's fingers with the alternate picking style:

2

The following exercises (5 - 7) are designed to go from an up-pick on one string to a down-pick on the adjacent string.

These next exercises (8 and 9) deal with parallel 4ths (8) and 7ths (9).

This exercise deals with the part of the neck where chromatic (½ step to ½ step) intervals are easily played.

Practice this exercise transposing up whole step to whole step.

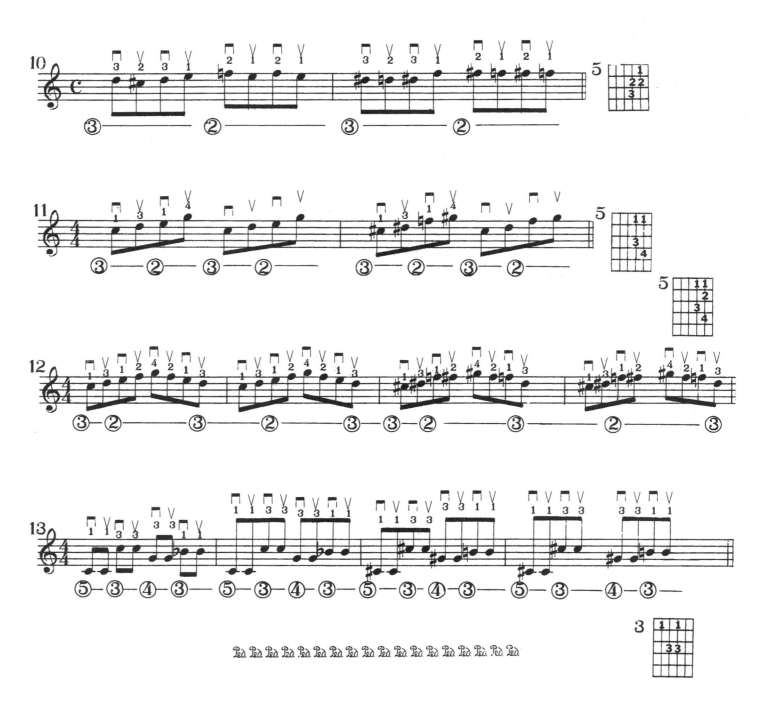

One day I was talking to a couple of musicians that do the Gong show. They said that the show was looking for talent among players in Los Angeles. I told them I was interested in doing the show. I went to the audition wearing a pink ballerina Tu Tu and played my guitar and sang. They scheduled me for a show that afternoon. I was not allowed to roam the halls of NBC. I had to stay in the room with the other contestants. It was sure bedlam in the room. How I survived the 4 hour wait I don't know but it turned out to be well worth it. I won the talent show. I received $532.10 for winning. They had to pay me $112.00 for being a member of the musicians union and I also received $150 for the use of the song (which I wrote) from BMI . . . . Lucrative pay for a dumb joke.

ECONOMY PICKING

This is a method I occasionally use in my playing. When I play on one string, I use alternate picking (⊓ + ∨). When I go to the next high adjacent string I always start with a down pick. I never deviate from this pattern until I go backwards from high to low string. Going backwards I use alternate picking. This picking technique minimizes energy in hand movement by using one pick stroke to cross from one string to next highest string.

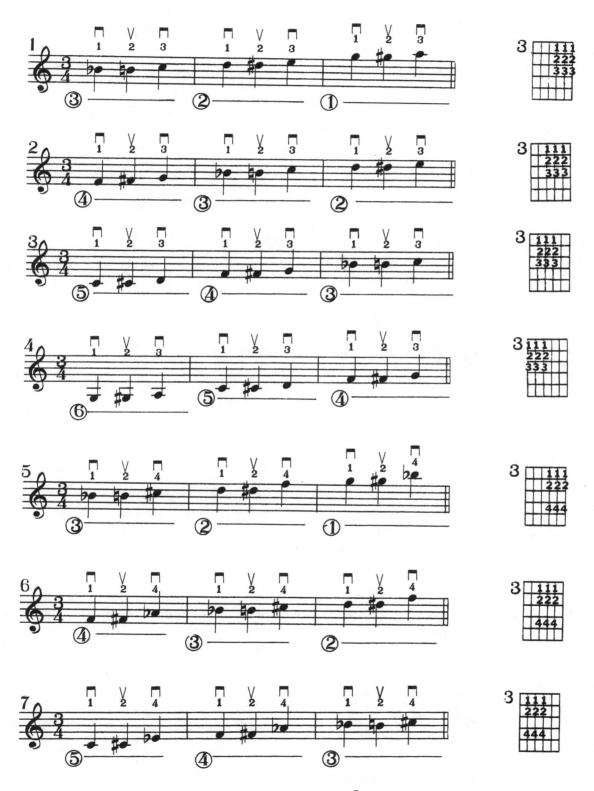

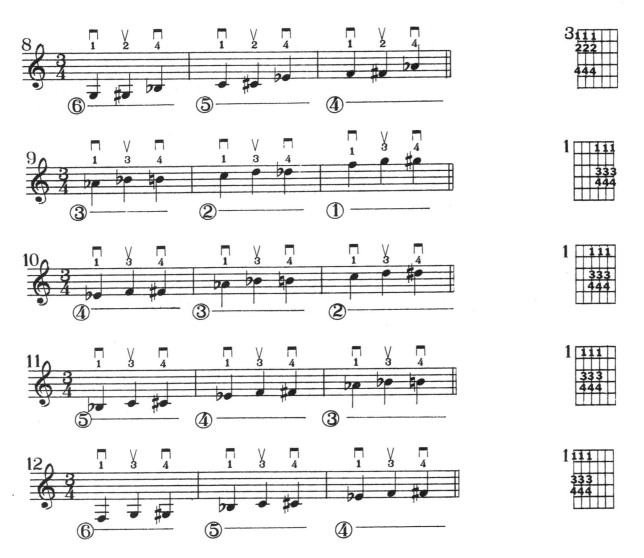

This exercise shows an economy pattern with a crossover down stroke that covers three adjacent strings (transpose pattern going chromatically up neck):

The exercise below demonstrates a picking pattern with two down-strokes and one up-stroke. The trick is to make these strokes into three even notes.

After completion, try this basic finger pattern on two other adjacent strings.

In the late 1960's I was doing a record album for Producer Mike Nesmith (of the Monkey's fame). The leader was Shorty Rogers. On one tune they asked the musicians to play very free sounds on the last chorus. Ad lib anything they wanted. When they came to this part, I turned the volume all the way up on my amplifier. I then threw my guitar up in the air. When the guitar hit the floor, strings popped, pegs broke, and a horrible sound came out of the amp. The whole orchestra started laughing and you could hear remarks like, "Tom's wild, Tedesco's crazy," etc. To my surprise, when the album was released, they left all this craziness in. Six months later I read an interview about the album with Mike Nesmith. He said, "One fellow, Tommy Tedesco, knew what we were after in the album." (Surprise.)

P.S. The band had to rest after this tune to enable me to go and get another guitar to finish the date. Everyone autographed my guitar and I put it into retirement.

ECONOMY PICKING FOR RUNS

I use this style for fast runs. I play my runs making sure there are three notes on each string. By using three notes on a string, the run comes out with a very systematic even approach. By keeping away from a picking pattern that's geared to a scale form with one or two notes on a string, my runs become standardized technique-wise. (These are examples of the runs used on the Tommy Garrett and 50 Guitar albums.)

A minor 9   Also works for: A minor 7, A minor 11,
              A minor, C major, C sixth, C Major 7

G7♭9   Also works for: G13♭9, G7♭13, G augmented, F diminished 7,
         A♭ diminished 7, B diminished 7, D diminished 7

C7   Also works for: C7♭5, B7♭9, A minor, A minor 7, A minor 9

7

A few years ago I had the call to do a week at the Los Angeles Greek Theater with Vicki Carr. They were also going to record every night which made it a lucrative job. I had a 5 minute solo on Spanish guitar behind Vicki's vocal which came out dynamite. "Leverage for me." After the second night the manager told me they didn't want me to smoke on stage. My compromise was to leave the stage for three numbers that I didn't have parts for. They agreed. They didn't realize the mistake they made until show night, when the people in the audience kept seeing the fat guitar player crawling thru the brass section three times a night, going backstage. A few weeks later I got a call to do a record date in a studio. Vicki sent the call out saying there will be NO SMOKING on the date. My message was, "NO SMOKING" - "NO TEDESCO." finis . . . . .

TREMOLO STUDY

The following exercise is a more systematic approach to tremolo study. Start the 16th note exercises slowly and build up the speed gradually until a tremolo sound starts happening. The changing of the note in the fourth beat of each phrase enables you to still feel control of the pick even though a tremolo is developing. A few different ways you will see a tremolo asked for are:

Tremolo   *Tremolo*   *Tremolo*

By practicing tremolos with this approach your pick hand uses the same technique for a tremolo as you would for reading any other type of music. Many guitarists use a stiff wrist for a tremolo even though they would not if they were reading 16th notes. It's much easier if you use your ordinary technique in tremolo situations.

Many years ago when I was doing all the Phil Spector dates there was a young fellow and his girl friend that used to come on the dates. Once in a while Phil would have the fellow play the tambourine on the date to make a few extra bucks. Occasionally the young man would run errands for Phil but not for the musicians. The girl friend was very shy. I sure didn't play my cards right because I had no idea that SONNY and CHER would make it so big.

MAJOR SCALES

These are the six scale positions for major scales I use. The notes in parentheses are notes found in the scale but are too few to make up a complete scale. All notes which are in the scale and that are accessible in that particular position are listed:

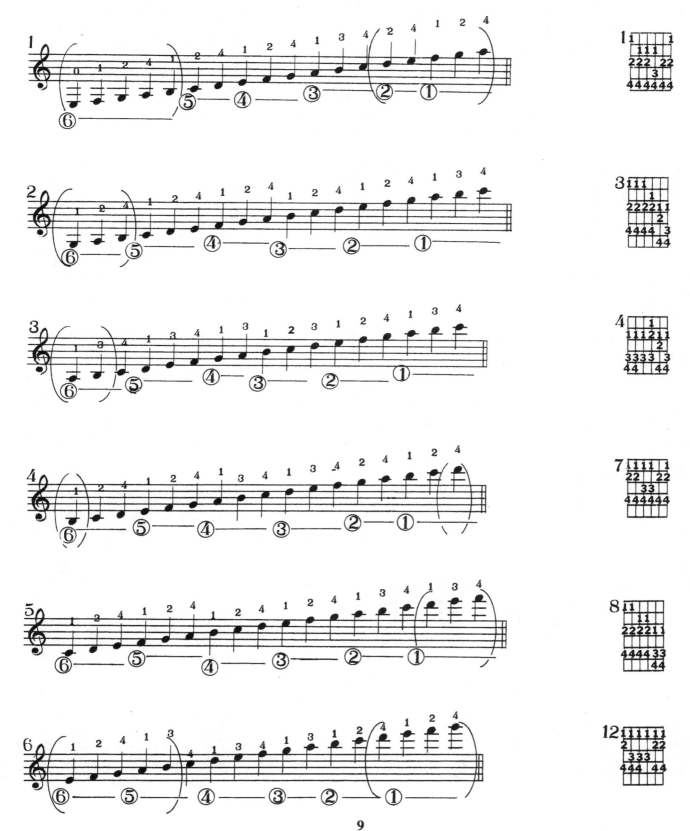

I was recording for Lou Rawls years ago with H. B. Barnum as leader. A few weeks before H. B. had challenged me to a foot race. During the date I reminded H. B. of the challenge and we decided to do it right then. Lou Rawls, H. B., myself and all the musicians went to the parking lot in back of Capitol Records during a break and walked off 100 yards. I knew I was in trouble when H. B. went to his car and came back with racing shoes. I talked him into a few yard spot for myself. It didn't mean a thing. When the race was over, H. B. could have given me a 50 yard lead and he still would have won. As I paid out all my bets to H. B. and the rest of the guys, I finally realized I was the conned one instead of being the connee!!!

🎵 🎵 🎵 🎵 🎵 🎵 🎵 🎵 🎵 🎵 🎵 🎵 🎵 🎵 🎵 🎵 🎵 🎵

MINOR SCALES
NATURAL MINOR SCALE

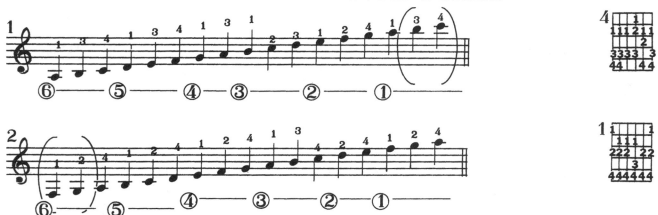

HARMONIC MINOR SCALE

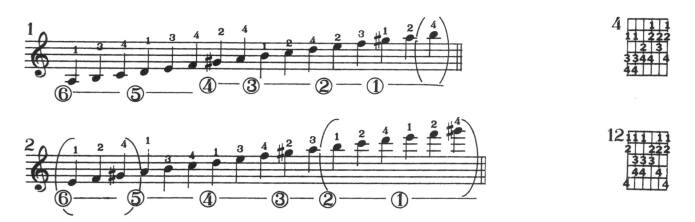

🎵 🎵 🎵 🎵 🎵 🎵 🎵 🎵 🎵 🎵 🎵 🎵 🎵 🎵 🎵 🎵 🎵 🎵

One day I over-dubbed some mandolin and miscellaneous other instruments on a Kenny Loggins record. While I was listening to the playback of the basic track, I commented, "Do you want me to continue playing when the 'chick' stops singing?" It became very quiet in the studio. The leader told me that wasn't a 'chick', that was Kenny Loggins singing. I looked at Kenny and tried to double talk my way out of this predicament but the look in his eyes assured me I was not successful.

🎵 🎵 🎵 🎵 🎵 🎵 🎵 🎵 🎵 🎵 🎵 🎵 🎵 🎵 🎵 🎵 🎵 🎵

MINOR SCALES CONTINUED

The last minor scale is the melodic minor. It ascends like a minor scale until the 5th step. Then it continues like a major scale. Descending, you must play a natural minor scale.

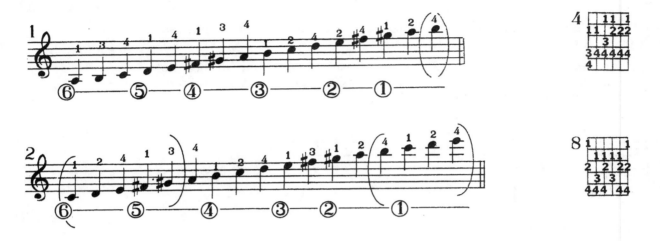

Many years ago I got a call to do some record dates with Frank Zappa. I had never worked with him before or met him; all I knew about him was the image he had created. I decided to be funny, so I showed up at the studio in an Indian costume, no shoes, and a golf hat. Frank came up and introduced himself and complimented me on my costume. I complimented him on his. I was sorry I went through this when I saw the guitar parts — they were as difficult as any I have ever played. After a struggling three hours, I went to Frank and told him how much I enjoyed his music and added that it was nothing like I had expected.

OTHER SCALES

The following are more scales you will encounter in your musical career. Besides reading them, try to memorize them:

1. Pentatonic scale
2. Whole tone scale
3. Diminished scale
4. Chromatic scale

This first scale you will encounter in rock-type writing (and Jazz also) is called the pentatonic scale (five steps per octave).

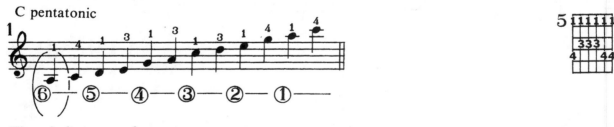

The whole tone scale:

In any form of augmented chords, (7b13's also) the writer may frequently employ the whole tone scale:

Note — Since this scale is symmetrical, (notes are one whole step apart from each other) there are just two whole tone scales.

The diminished scale is used by writers over diminished chords, and 7th chords of the dominant nature (for dom. 7ths the scale is played ½ step higher than the 7th chord). Here is a position version and an elongated version:

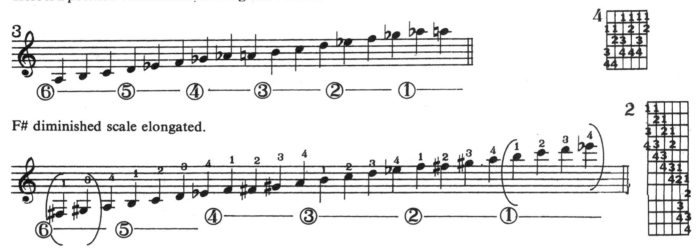

F# diminished scale elongated.

You will notice the diminished scale maintains a whole step to half step relationship throughout. Therefore, the scale repeats itself every four frets (minor 3rd) just like the diminished chord. Thus, there are only three diminished scales to learn.

each scale outlines three other related scales all a minor 3rd apart	F# A C Eb	Gb Bb Db E	G# B D F

This scale is the chromatic scale. Since every note is ½ step apart, there isn't really a tone center. This scale will usually be found as some kind of run, so practice it in all positions.

Notice that the last "a" is played with 4th finger again. Upon descending, start with the 4th finger on "A". Proceed without sliding the 4th finger to "Ab". This will bring your pattern up one fret, leaving you with an A#, first finger at the bottom string. Now slide to A, using your first finger.

SIGHT READING SECTION

14

I was working at a night club on the Sunset Strip in the late 50's backing singer Bobby Darin. Being a true sports fanatic I had my transistor radio with me listening to the Dodger game while the show was going on. Naturally I was using an ear plug. During one of the songs the ear plug fell out and the sports announcer's voice could be heard throughout the club. Bobby looked back at the band with a look that could kill. After the show, Bobby screamed at the conductor for allowing this to go on. (I don't remember if the Dodgers won or lost.)

LEARNING THE NOTES ON THE GUITAR

Most guitar players seem to rely on position playing (1st position, 2nd position, etc.) in their sight reading technique. As soon as they see notes not played in a particular position, many times they are stuck. In reality they really do not know the notes on the guitar fingerboard. You will notice in the chart, I show all the notes used in practical playing, followed by exercises to get you accustomed to seeing the notes. Each exercise uses only one string at a time. Don't worry if there are big skips. The exercises are primarily for finding a particular note on a particular string.

NOTES ON STRINGS

(numbers above notes show frets)

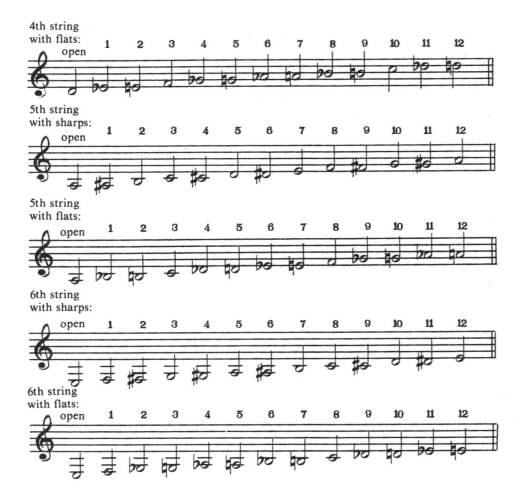

4th string with flats:
5th string with sharps:
5th string with flats:
6th string with sharps:
6th string with flats:

NOTES ON FIRST STRING

(from Open to 15th fret)

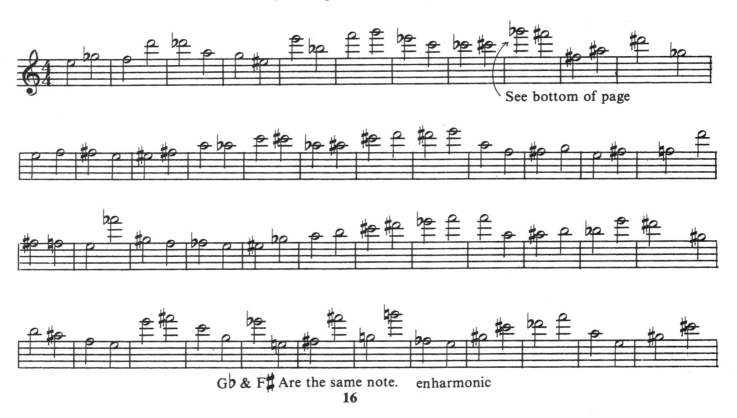

See bottom of page

G♭ & F♯ Are the same note.   enharmonic

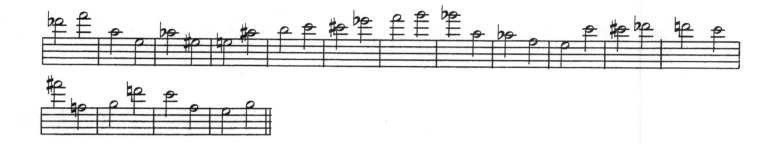

NOTES ON SECOND STRING

(from Open to 15th fret)

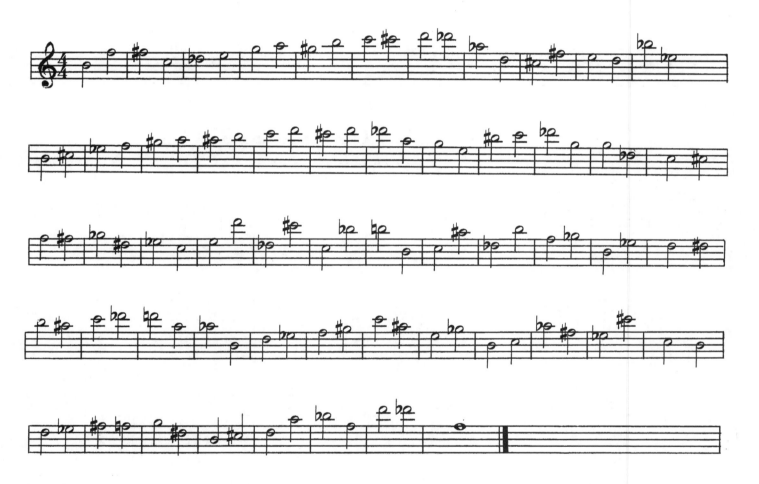

NOTES ON THIRD STRING

(from Open to 12th fret)

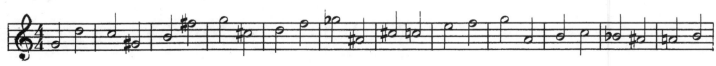

NOTES ON FOURTH STRING

(from Open to 12th fret)

NOTES ON FIFTH STRING

(from Open to 12th fret)

NOTES ON SIXTH STRING

(from Open to 12th fret)

TIME FIGURES

For the student just learning to read on the guitar, let me show you the method I use for reading time figures. Always count to yourself until the reading of certain passages are automatic.

NOTE VALUES

Tie ⌣ - a curved line used to connect two notes of the same musical pitch. Do not strike note; it is only a continuation of the first.

REST VALUES

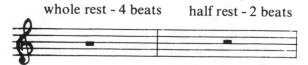

whole rest - 4 beats   half rest - 2 beats

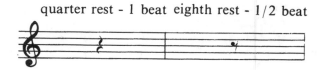

quarter rest - 1 beat   eighth rest - 1/2 beat

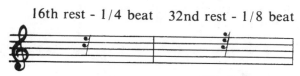

16th rest - 1/4 beat   32nd rest - 1/8 beat

TIME SIGNATURES

TIME SIGNATURE: At the beginning of a piece we have the time signature. The lower figure indicates what note receives a beat (4 - quarter note; 8 - eighth note; 2 - half note). The upper indicates how many to a bar (4/4 - quarter gets a beat - 4 beats to a bar); (3/8 - eighth gets a beat - 3 beats to a bar).

MIXING TIME AND RESTS

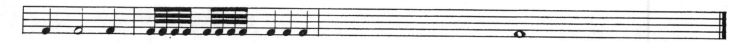

I was working for Wes Farrel, the Producer of the Partridge Family. The other guitar player on the date was Louie Shelton. At one part of the date I was helping Louie on his part (Louie was a great player but a novice reader on guitar.) Wes came out of the booth and yelled for us to be quiet. I explained I was helping Louie with his part. He said, "Fine, go ahead and help him." Because of his attitude, I said, "Forget it, everyone's on their own." They spent the next 15 minutes helping Louie with his part. I refused . . . Needless to say, this was a mutual goodbye date for Wes Farrel.

21

I was doing a date for Hank Mancini a few years ago. On the date was Shelly Manne on drums and Pete and Conti Condoli on trumpets. Pete played a beautiful trumpet solo on one tune. The rhythm section could not see the soloist from where we were sitting. Shelly remarked to me what a beautiful solo Conti just played. (Shelly wasn't aware it was Pete's solo.) I decided to put him on. I told him he really must know the sound of Conti's playing since Conti has worked for years with Shelly's group. Shelly came back with smug remarks such as, "I know Conti's playing like my own. When you are a jazz player, you know, nobody has a jazz feel like Conti, etc." You can imagine Shelly's embarrassment when I told him it was Pete's solo. I haven't let up on Shelly since. (Many people hear music with their eyes instead of their ears.)

EXERCISES ON 1ST, 2ND, 3RD AND 4TH STRING

The following are exercises I have developed to make you more familiar with the guitar notes on the fingerboard. Don't worry about tempo or timing. They are mainly there to get your fingers moving up and down the fingerboard. Follow the instructions on the top of each exercise. (Exercise on 1st and 2nd string, exercises on 2nd and 3rd string, etc.)

Try to recognize repeated intervals that can move up and down the fingerboard without changing fingering. Example below.

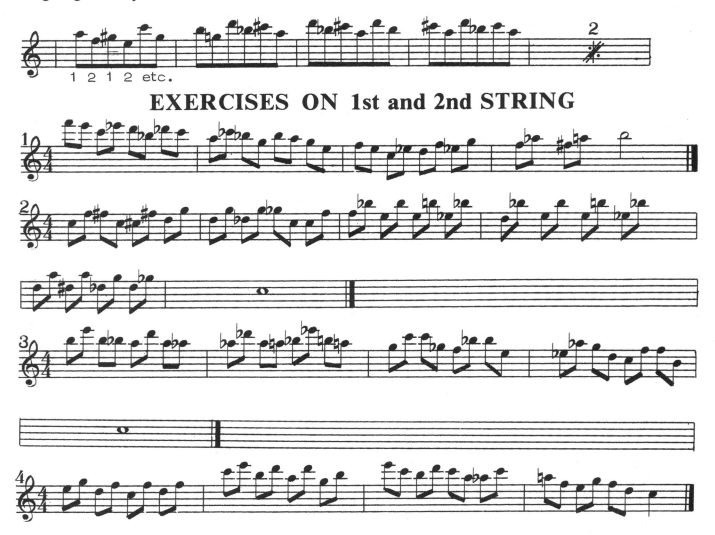

EXERCISES ON 1st and 2nd STRING

22

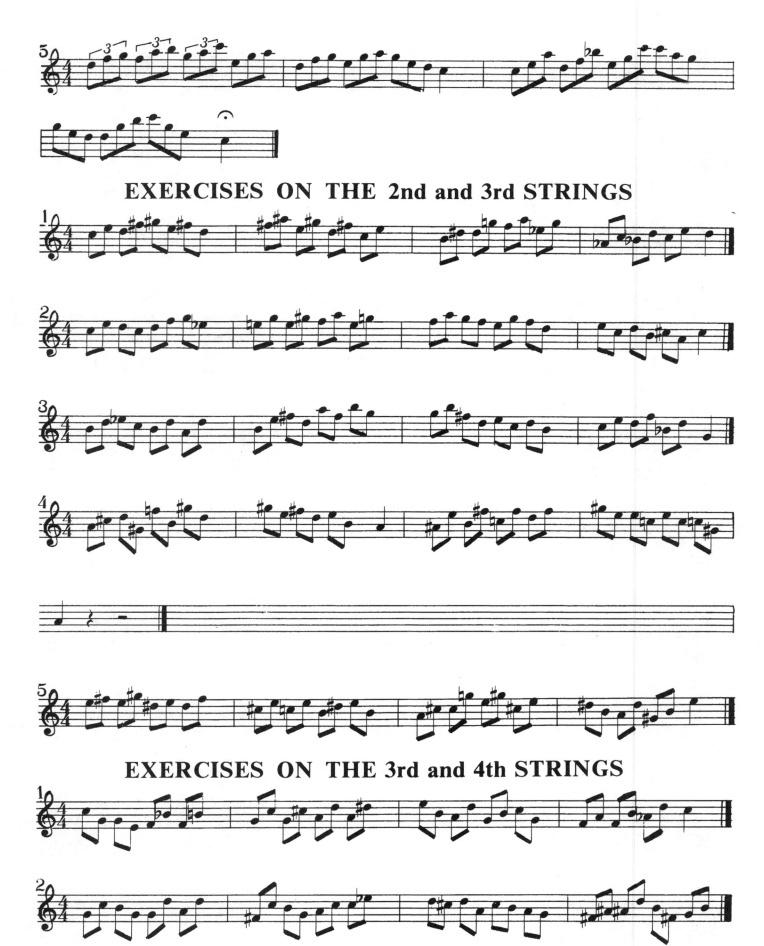

EXERCISES ON THE 2nd and 3rd STRINGS

EXERCISES ON THE 3rd and 4th STRINGS

EXERCISES ON THE 1st, 2nd and 3rd STRINGS

SOLO USING 1st, 2nd, 3rd and 4th STRINGS

LOW NOTE READING

Low note reading is generally not as difficult as high note reading. Primarily because after you begin to recognize the low notes, all your surrounding notes are notes that are familiar to you.

LOW READING

LOW READING

27

LOW READING

POSITION PLAYING EXERCISES

You will notice the next nine (9) exercises are all written with no sharps or flats in any key signature. However, they all have different tonalities. I purposely didn't put the correct key signatures in to let you constantly see the notes you will be playing on the guitar. After a while your fingers will go automatically to a note just like a typist types without thinking of letters or numbers. Before each exercise, check position noted on top of music.

SCALE EXAMPLE IN 1st POSITION

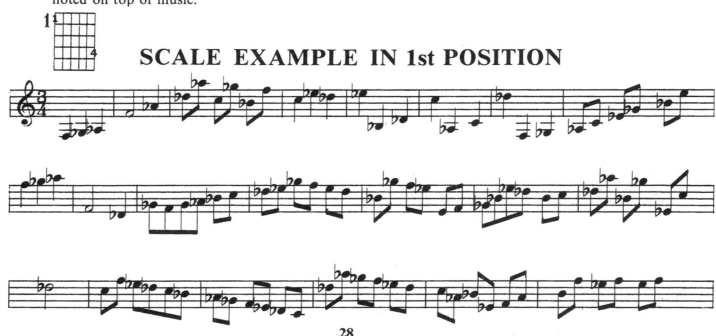

SCALE EXAMPLE IN 2nd POSITION

SCALE EXAMPLES IN 3rd POSITION

SCALE EXAMPLES IN 4th POSITION

30

SCALE EXAMPLES IN 5th POSITION

SCALE EXAMPLES IN 7th POSITION

SCALE EXAMPLES IN 8th POSITION

SCALE EXAMPLES IN 9th POSITION

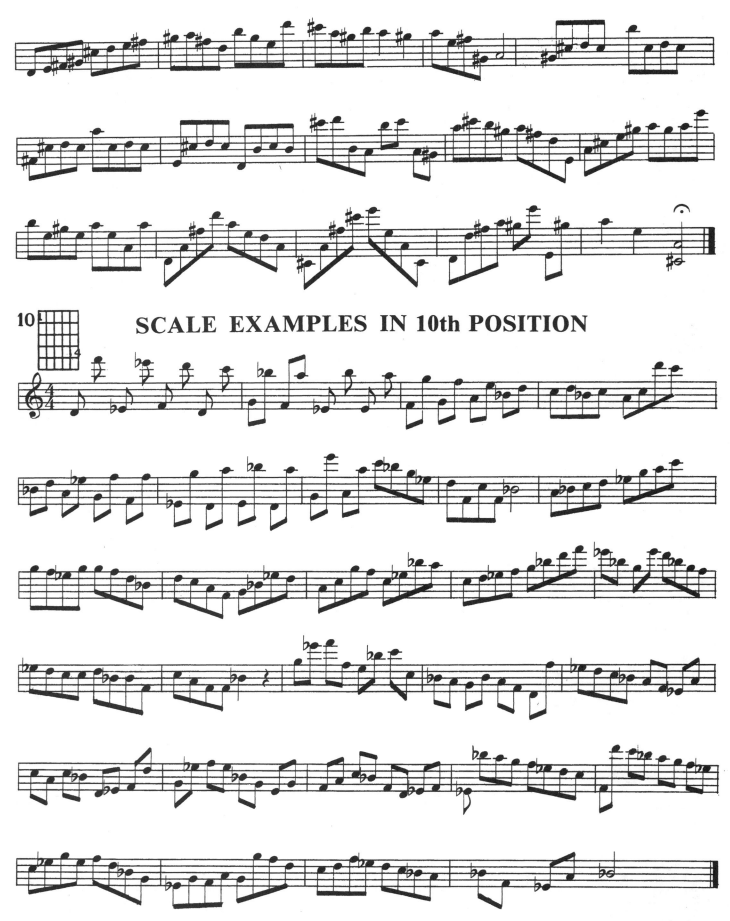

SCALE EXAMPLES IN 10th POSITION

A couple of years ago I was doing a record date with Herb Alpert and the Tijuana Brass. I had been working furiously for a few days and was utterly exhausted. After we came back from lunch and started the second date I could hardly keep my eyes open. I remembered Herbie telling me a few weeks before about this restaurant near the studio where his son ate and got sick. I went to Herb and told him I was sick maybe from the food I just ate at the restaurant down the street. He told me the same thing happened to his son recently. (He didn't remember telling me the story before.) He volunteered to play guitar on the next tune so I could lie down and rest. After an hour's nap I came back ready for action. Herb didn't know about my invented story. (Till now that is . . .)

HIGH NOTE READING

Many students find high note reading a problem. Even after they learn to recognize the high notes, a problem still exists. This is because all the surrounding notes are in a foreign area to the student. When doing the following exercises, try to keep all notes played in high positions to get you used to seeing them there.

HIGH READING

HIGH READING

HIGH READING

HIGH READING

37

A few years ago when Lee Ritenour started his recording career I used to kid him about being too cocky. A situation came about a little later when I was able to use the Tedesco charm - (voodoo). We were doing a movie with David Schire at Warner Bros. On one tune Lee had a picking solo alone for 16 bars before the orchestra came in. He did a beautiful job. He looked at me with the cocky look. I decided to work him over. I said, "I'll bet you a dollar you don't play it perfect on the first take." He accepted my challenge. As the room quieted down for the take, I reminded him of the whole orchestra listening to him. "Beware of the finger noise on the guitar; be sure to be with the conductor." Sure enough, after the third bar he blew it. I asked him if he would like to bet another dollar on the second take. He accepted. I reminded him of how much harder it would be now after goofing the first take. Sure enough, he blew it. I looked at him and he had a pale look. I told him no more bets, just play the part. He did the part and I took his two dollars and bought his lunch. "Mission Accomplished."

CHORD FORM READING

Many times in reading single notes, chord forms start to appear. This makes the notes more recognizable to a player.

You will notice in Exercise 1 immediately chord forms appear.

Bar 1 - G chord
Bar 2 - Em chord
Bar 3 - Am chord
Bar 3A - C chord

Throughout all these exercises you will notice all different chord forms. Major, Minor, Diminished, etc. Experiment putting them in different places on the guitar.

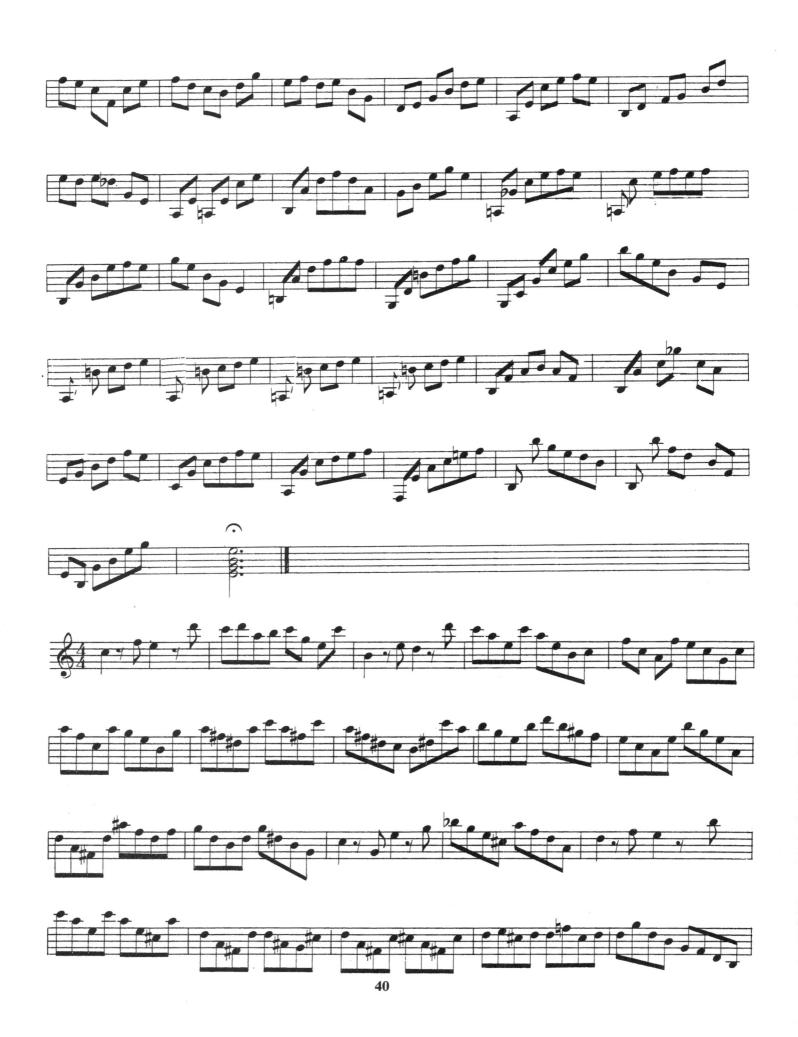

41

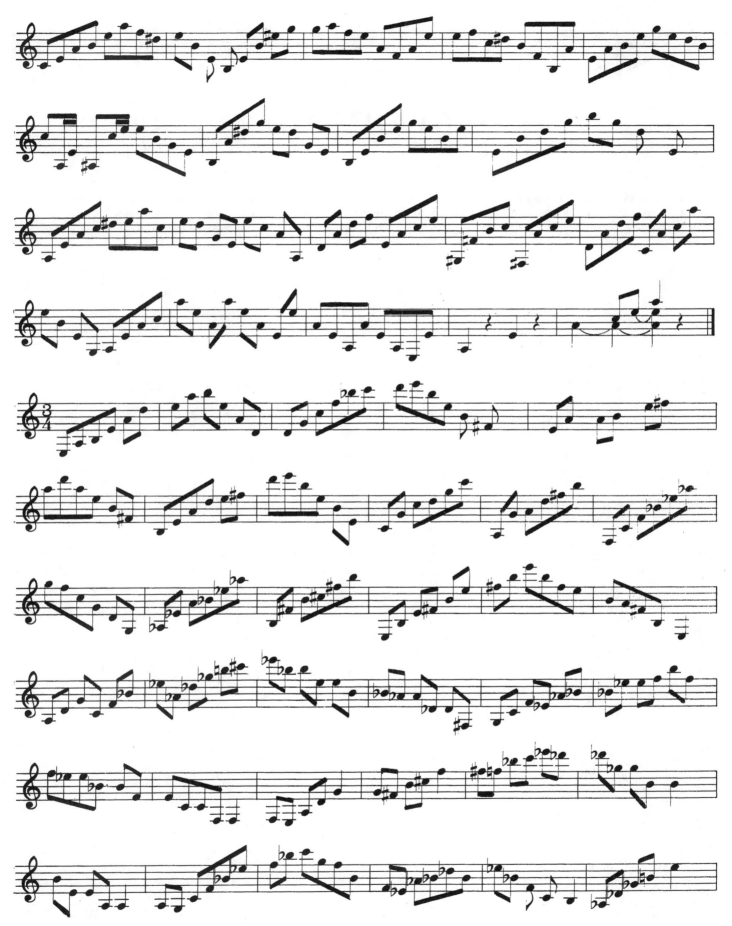

43

SYNCOPATION

Syncopation in music is the temporary displacement of the natural accent. To help me in reading syncopation I use the various 1 &, 1 & ah, 1 e & ah, etc. principles. To be a good sight reader in syncopated time you must learn and play a figure until it is second nature. This figure should not be a problem again. Your memory bank will make you play the figure correctly in the future. Even after 40 years of playing guitar, I still see new figures. I analyze the new figure and try to remember it for the next time. Below you will find a few figures that will appear constantly in syncopated reading. Memorize each one for the future.

Refer to time figure section.

44

47

Universal Studios called Larry Carlton and myself to do a TV film. It was supposed to be a "now" type music score. On one of the cues Larry played some beautiful fills. The leader didn't seem to like it. He said he wanted it to sound more Rock and Roll. He didn't understand the good sound Larry was producing. To the leader, Rock and Roll is bad playing. I turned my amp up to "10". I used Fuzz, Wa Wa, and attacked. It was so horrible the leader loved it. I looked at Larry and jokingly told him he didn't know anything about Rock and Roll. Larry just shook his head in disbelief. Score another one for music business versus music.

POSITION CHANGING

Many times a song may start out in the key of C and by the time you are through with this song, you will have modulated through three (3) or four (4) different keys. The use of accidentals will throw you into a new key before you might even be aware of it. The following music is an example of this. When I am reading this type of an arrangement and I see many flats appearing, I automatically try to bring my left hand to the 1st, 3rd, 5th, 6th, or 8th position. If I see many sharps my left hand goes to the 2nd, 4th, 6th, 7th, or 9th position. Although this is not a foolproof method, it has worked for me more times than not.

For instance:

    Bar 2 - Flats - 5th position
    Bar 10 - Sharps - 2nd position
    Bar 16 - Flats - 1st position
    Bar 18 - Sharps - 4th position
    Bar 25 - Flats - 1st position
    Bar 28 - Sharps - 2nd position
    Bar 32 - Flats - 3rd position

If you practice these bars, you will notice your fingers will lie very comfortably playing the part. After you have been playing for a while, your eyes and hands will search out these positions on the guitar automatically.

A few years ago I worked for a leader who was considered a tyrant. I had never worked for him before, so I was looking forward to the call. (I don't know why, but I look forward to these types of challenges.) Sure enough, half way through the date he screamed at me: "You are supposed to be playing in unison with the cellos. You are behind them. Listen to the cellos." I decided right then what I would do. He started the next take, and when this passage came up, I didn't play. He leered at me and screamed: "Why didn't you play?" I gave him one of my very silly looks and said, "But I thought you wanted me to listen to the cellos." A big silence hit the band, expecting him to fly in a fit of rage, but instead he smiled and said, "Please play this time." I escaped again!

OTHER TIME SIGNATURES

In dealing with other time signatures besides 4/4 and 3/4, the underlying principle rule of a time signature stays the same. The bottom note tells what note gets a beat. The top note tells how many beats in a measure.

Just remember, the value of each note stays relative to each other (a quarter note gets a beat, so the eighth note gets a half-beat). (The eighth note gets a beat, so the quarter note gets two beats.)

The same principle goes for all the other notes.

EXAMPLE:
16th note is ½ value of eighth note, which is
½ value of a quarter note, which is
½ value of a half note, which is
½ value of a whole note

The following musical examples will get you used to reading in different time signatures.

51

OTHER TIME SIGNATURES

D.S. al coda

One day I arrived at CBS for a date for George Roumanis and discovered I left my electric guitar at home. Instead of panicking like a novice, I played the score on Bass guitar "8VA" up. I was a nervous wreck until my wife arrived with my electric guitar. In the meantime, not a moment of music scoring was lost because of my error. A younger non-experienced player would have told them he didn't have his guitar and they would have waited maybe an hour or so before they could record. That would have been the end of this musician with any leader. Moments wasted in this business is very costly.

COMBINING TIME SIGNATURES

In combining time signatures where the bottom number is the same and the top number is different, (3/4 to 5/4, or 2/4 to 4/4, 7/4 to 2/4, 9/4 to 7/4) there is no real problem. A quarter note still gets a beat and the top figure tells how many beats in the measure. Examples of this are exercise #1, where we go from 3/4 to 2/4. The problems might arise when we combine figures where the bottom number is different. (4/4 to 3/8, 6/4 to 5/8, 3/4 to 7/8) Here we have to remember that the eighth notes still receive half the value of quarter notes. Example is exercise #2 where we go from 2/4 to 3/8, 5/8 to 7/8. The value of the eighth notes stay the same.

I have had a habit for years whenever I have a part that has all rests and the one note or chord on the last bar of the tune; I fold the part, put it in my pocket and go and relax. My theory is the whole orchestra has the note and they don't need my help. One day at MGM, I was doing a movie for composer, Lalo Schifrin. The fourth cue was very long and tacit the guitar until the last bar. Naturally I folded the part and went to have coffee. Ten minutes later they tracked me down and said they needed me for this cue. They had been looking all over for me. I went back and said I didn't have a part. (Tedesco's white lie . . .) It turned out the last chord was a suspense chord with guitar alone. I NOW always sit thru one rehearsal of the part. (Then I fold up the part and hang out.)

PICK AND FINGERS

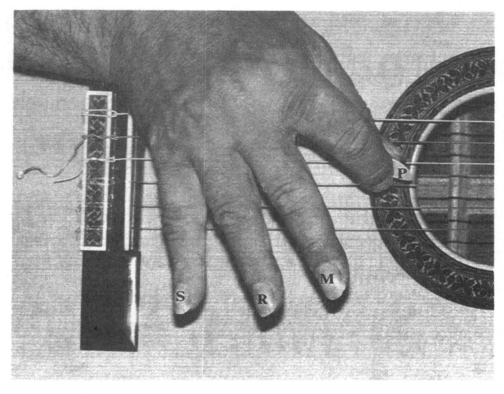

S = Small   R = Ring   M = Middle   P = Pick

Sometimes in music I have to use both my pick and fingers to play a part. I use primarily my middle finger and ring finger to do the extra notes. In a pinch I will use my small finger. Try the following five exercises with the fingers I have marked. Then try them with your own fingering.

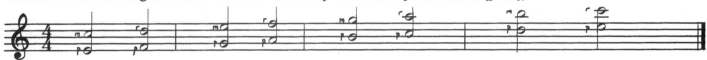

PICK AND FINGER EXERCISE

Try the following exercise using your own fingering.

rit.

FINGERPICKING

On a Universal call for Mike Post and Pete Carpenter there was a new guitarist by the name of John Wheelock. It was his first job in town. After I met him I looked at the guitar parts and gave him guitar 1 and I took guitar 2. I told him I had a hard time sight reading and kept asking him for his advice throughout the date. The conversation seemed to relax him and he came through successfully. A few years later he thanked me for the way that first date went even though he found out later I had been putting him on about the reading. He was thankful I gave him the opportunity to play the lead parts to show his capabilities.

VERTICAL CHORD READING

In much of my work vertical chord reading is essential. When playing these parts, get whatever you can comfortably the first time. The next time, build on whatever you did the first time. By the third time you will have most of the notes in your grasp. Try to read chords from the top note down. Your top note is usually the most important part of the chord. This also gives you a leeway if you don't play all the notes; the leader will hear the important top melody note.

See bottom of page

* Use open strings as much as possible in these types of musical exercises.

66

68

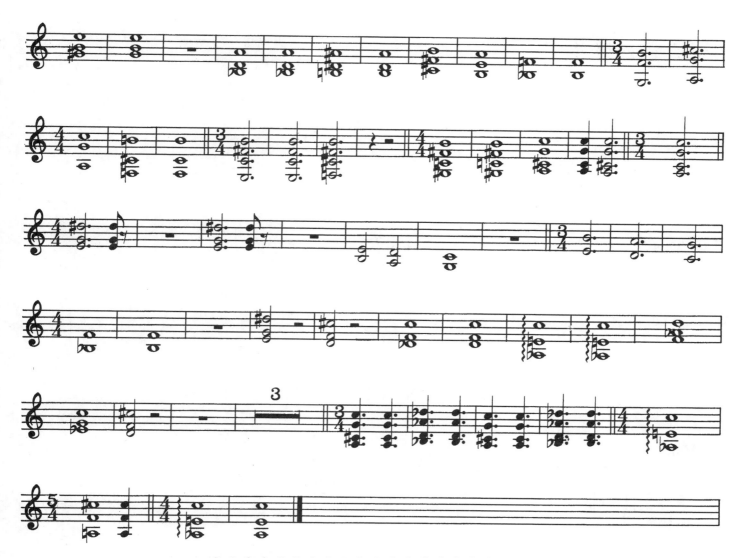

Last year I had a movie score with Jerry Goldsmith. On a couple of contemporary type cues he hired a young ex guitar player to write for this style. The young orchestrator beamed when he went to the podium. On the ending of one cue he looked at me and said, "Tom, that last chord is really out of tune." The second guitar player on the date was Lee Ritenour. I looked at Lee and told him to watch the happenings. I didn't touch the pegs on the guitar and looked at the leader and asked if this was better in tune. When I played the chord, he said it was much better and in tune. I looked at Lee and said, "I guess the leader has all the dialogue of a leader but not the ears of a musician."

CHORD SYMBOLS

Eighty per cent of the time when I am at work, I am seeing chord symbols rather than single notes. On the part will be notated the style wanted. Generally if they ask for a certain style, I will play what is more natural for the style rather than what is written.

CHORD SYMBOLS MOST OFTEN SEEN

C Major - C △ or C Maj. or CM

C diminished - C⁰, C dim

C Minor - C - , C min., Cm

C Dominant 7 - C7, C Seventh

C Minor 7 - C - 7, Cm7, C min 7

C minor-major 7 — C-7, C min. 7, E♭+/C

C Major 7 - C7, C Maj. 7, C △ 7, CM7

C Eleventh — C11, B♭/C, G-7/C, C7 sus 4

C diminished 7 - C⁰7, C dim 7

C half-diminished 7 - C∅, C∅7, C min 7♭5, A min. 6, C-7♭5

C augmented — C+, Caug., C+5, C △ #5

COMMON VOICINGS

a. C Major

b. C minor

c. C augmented

d. C dominant 7

COMMON VOICINGS CONTINUED

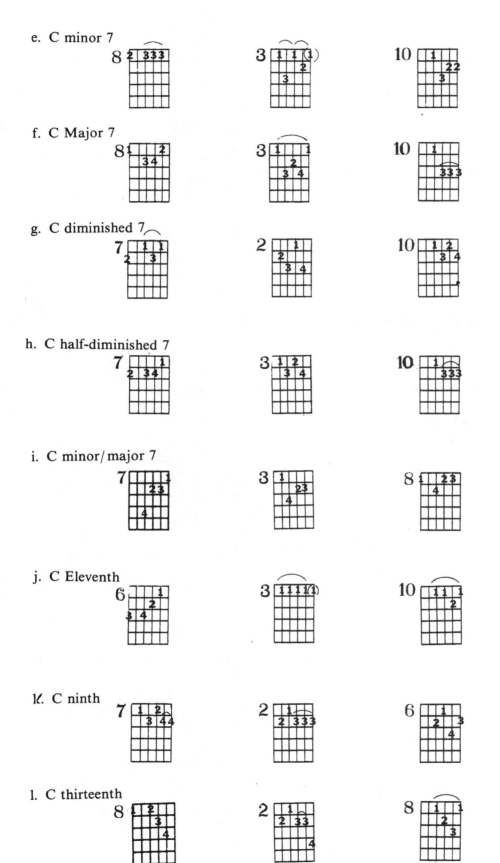

e. C minor 7

f. C Major 7

g. C diminished 7

h. C half-diminished 7

i. C minor/major 7

j. C Eleventh

k. C ninth

l. C thirteenth

71

m. C seventh b5

n. C seventh #5 (+5)

o. C seven b9

p. C seventh #9

VOICE LEADING

Frequently, a writer will notate common inner-moving voice figures with chord symbols instead of notation. These can be notated several different ways: with chord-slashes, chord symbols and notation.

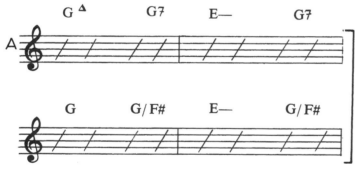

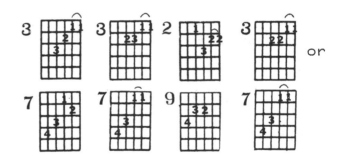

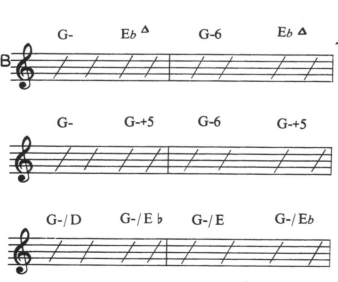

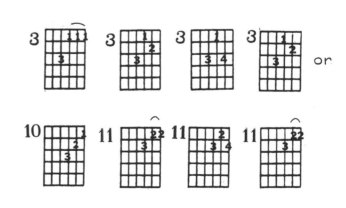

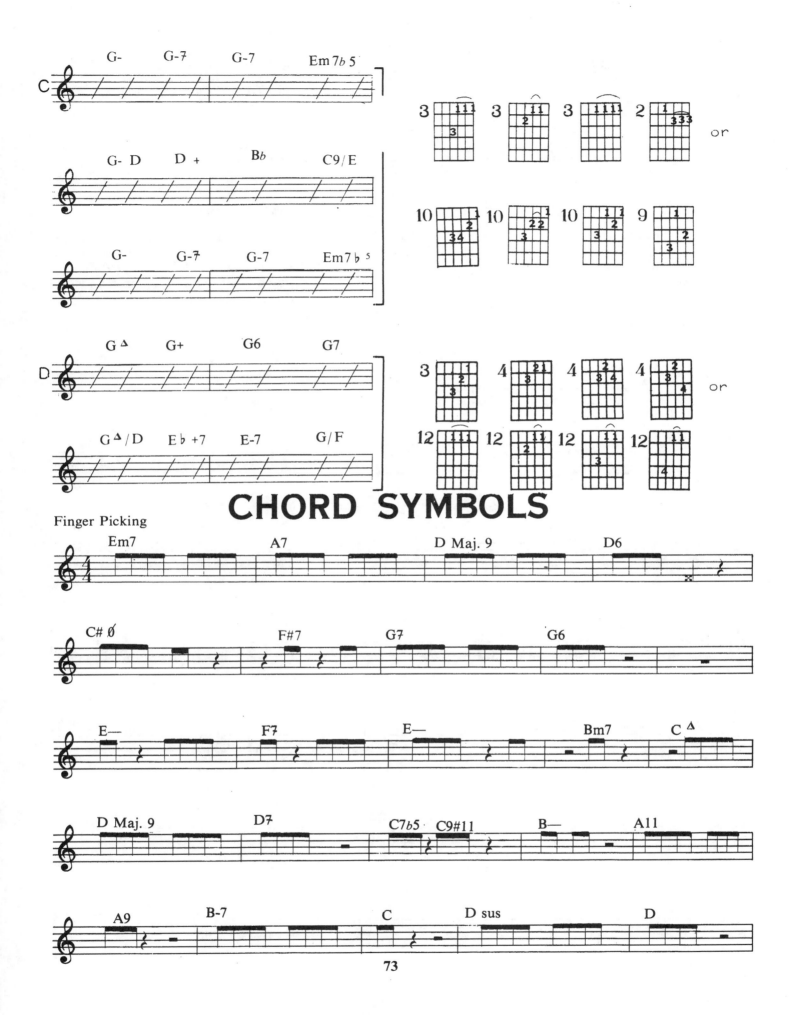

CHORD SYMBOLS

Finger Picking

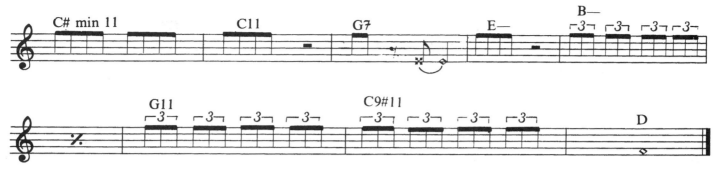

Years ago I was doing a Jan and Dean date for Lou Adler. During the date Lou's secretary came in and I asked her for the $50.00 they owed me for something I did a while back. She completely ignored me. I put my guitar down and stopped playing. I told Lou, Jan, and Dean I would not play until my $50.00 obligation was fulfilled. None of the fellows carried much cash so they were borrowing from the mixer, engineer, and whoever they could to get me the cash. They paid me and the date started back. After the date I took all the musicians out for dinner and blew all the money. I wanted to show it was the principle and not the money that bothered me. (My primmadonna period.)

CHORD SYMBOLS

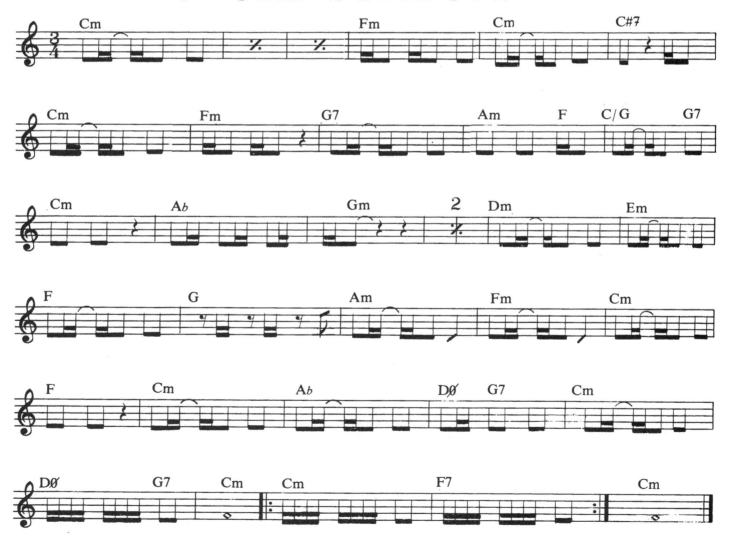

CHORD SYMBOLS

CHORD SYMBOLS

Flamenco Style or Spanish-like

CHORD SYMBOLS

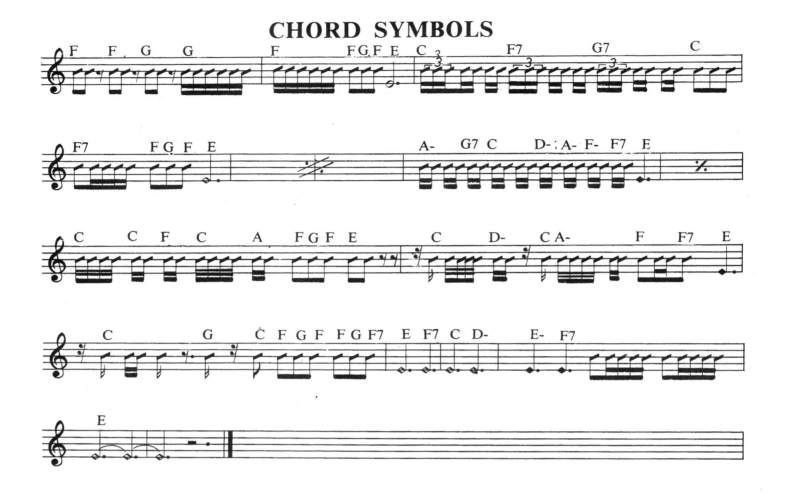

In 1960 guitarist Bill Pitman and myself worked with Paul Anka at the Coconut Grove for two (2) weeks. On one particular tune I had an eight (8) bar solo. Every night I would take requests from the members of the orchestra what they would like to hear in those eight (8) bars. Some of those requests were *Home on the Range, Happy Birthday, Star Spangled Banner,* etc. I tried to fit all these tunes into a rock style. The leader on the job, Sid Feller (who later became a good friend of mine) kept looking up at me each evening, not sure of what was happening.

Years ago when I was just starting in the business, I got a call from Bobby Gibbons to sub on a record date for him. The producer on the date was Harry Lubin when I showed up on the date. Harry was shocked and disturbed when he saw me. He wanted to know where Bobby was. I told him I didn't know but if he was unhappy, I would leave. He said to forget it and go ahead and set up and play. I started out with a solo that Lupin loved. He rushed out of the recording booth screaming, "I love what you're doing. I am sure glad you stayed." I asked Harry why he didn't wait to hear me play before he condemned me. He said, "You look like a shoe salesman, not a guitar player." I laughed at his remark and ended up working on dates for Harry for many years to come.

STUDIO SECTION

LOS ANGELES CHAPTER
THE NATIONAL ACADEMY OF RECORDING ARTS & SCIENCES

presents

Tommy Tedesco

this

MOST VALUABLE PLAYER AWARD

for consistently outstanding

performance as a

Guitarist

for the year 1974

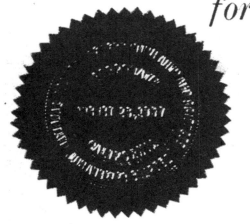

[signature]

PRESIDENT,
LOS ANGELES CHAPTER

A STUDIO PLAYER

Contrary to the popular belief, a player that works Studio jobs is not necessarily a Studio player. He might be a specialized player in a certain area and called upon to do his specialty on a date (rock, jazz, classical, country, etc.) If these players are miscast, which often happens, and they are thrown in circumstances foreign to their specialty, DISASTER STRIKES. When you take a job, be sure it is right for you. I will try to define Studio playing in five different categories and a brief description of each category.

1. Records
2. Jingles
3. TV film
4. Movies
5. Live TV shows

We have a saying in the studios. It goes like this. "Studio work is 95% boredom and 5% terror." Be prepared for the 5% terror and you will be able to fight off the 95% boredom.

I was doing a TV film and invited a young guitar player from New York, Marc Silvers, to sit and observe. He noticed my knee was resting against the back of my amplifier. He asked me why. I told him the gadget holding the fuse broke a couple of days before and I had to hold the fuse in to allow the amp to work. A few minutes later I had him holding the fuse in with his hands while I played a solo. He looked at me bewildered. He had always heard about the big studio player technique but this was not exactly what he had ever expected.

CONTRACTOR

A majority of your calls for Studio work will come from a Contractor. (A Contractor is a person appointed by the Studio or leader to hire a band.) The Contractor is a powerful figure in the music business. He can help or hurt a musician's career. The leader will call his Contractor and say, "I need a band for a record date for Dec. 12 from 8 to 12 at R & R Studio. I need a guitar. Try guitar player A or guitar player B. If you cannot get them, get me someone of their caliber. If the guitar players A or B cannot make the date, the power of the Contractor comes into being. He uses his own discretion on who to hire. He hopes his judgment is the best. If he has a new good player on hand, he will help him to get the job. It is best to keep on good terms with a Contractor. (I've made a few mistakes in my day.)

While I was writing this book, I spoke to a few Contractors in regards to hiring of new unproven musicians. I asked them all the same questions. Below you will find the questions and their answers.

QUESTION:

1. When do you hire new unproven musicians?

ANSWERS:

1. We hire new players generally when the players we usually use are busy and we need a player to fill the job.

2. We hear through the grape-vine about a player doing great work for other people but we haven't had the occasion to try him ourselves.

3. An established player will come to us and recommend a new player that meets Studio work qualifications.

4. When a leader asks for him.

QUESTION:

2. How do you go about hiring these new players?

ANSWERS:

1. We check with the more experienced players in regards to the new player's qualifications.

2. We will ask the new player about his previous jobs and experience.

3. We will check with leaders the new players have worked for to verify their qualifications.

QUESTION:
3. What do you expect from a new player that you hire?

ANSWERS:

1. To be on time.

2. Good conduct.

3. Pay attention.

4. No wisecracks.

5. Just sit and play.

6. Have the necessary instruments for the job (acoustic guitar, electric guitar, nylon string guitar, 12 string guitar, etc.) Whatever is needed for that particular job.

7. Don't accept the job if the player feels he isn't ready.

8. Don't ask for extra money if you are a new player on the scene. (Even though premium money to experienced players is paid, a Contractor feels you haven't been around long enough to join that league.)

DOUBLING

Doubling (the playing of different instruments) is an important part of the studio scene. Besides the aesthetic value of playing the correct instrument for each situation, doubling can be a bonanza for a guitar player in wages earned. The following chart shows how the doubles are figured in different studio categories:

MOVIES: Three (3) instruments played (i.e., acoustic, electric, and 12 string)
100% pay for the 1st instrument
50% extra for the 2nd instrument
20% extra for the 3rd and each subsequent instrument

TV FILM: Same as movies

RECORDS: Three (3) instruments played (i.e., nylon string, mandolin, and banjo)
100% pay for the 1st instrument
20% extra for the 2nd instrument
15% extra for the 3rd and each subsequent instrument

COMMERCIALS: Any three (3) instruments played
100% pay for the 1st instrument
30% extra for the 2nd instrument
15% extra for the 3rd and each subsequent instrument

LIVE TV: Any three (3) instruments played
100% pay for the 1st instrument
25% extra for the 2nd instrument
10% extra for the 3rd and each subsequent instrument

The following instruments are considered as doubles for guitar players:
Banjo - 4 string	Ukulele
Banjo - 5 string	Balalaika
Electric guitar	Banduria (Spanish mandolin)

Acoustic guitar	Bouzouki
Classical guitar	Bottle neck guitar
Bass guitar - 6 string	Lute
Bass guitar - 4 string	Mandola
Dobro guitar	Oud
Steel guitar	Riquinta
Tenor guitar (4 string)	Sitar
12 string guitar	Tiple
Mandolin	

The majority of the studio guitar players tune all the miscellaneous instruments to a guitar type tuning. Below I will give you a few examples of how I tune my instruments with string gauges I use on each instrument:

Banjo (4 string)
    1st string — E — .010
    2nd string — B — .015
    3rd string — G — .017
    4th string — D — .024 (wound)

Mandolin
    1st string (double string — E — .009
    2nd string (double string — B — .012
    3rd string (double string) — G — .017
    4th string (double string) — D — .024

Bouzouki
    1st string (double string — E — .010
    2nd string (double string — B — .013
    3rd string — (A) string — G — .022
    3rd string — (B) string — G — .009
    4th string — (A) string — D — .028
    4th string — (B) string — D — .011

Balalaika
    1st string — E — .010
    2nd string — B — .012
    3rd string — B — .013

MUSIC EXAMPLES FOR DOUBLING INSTRUMENTS

Type of parts you might see for banjo.

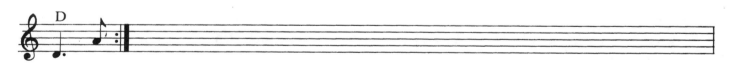

Type of parts you might see for mandolin.

Type of parts you might see for bouzouki.

CONDUCTING IN STUDIO WORK

Many times a good reading guitar player gets a crack at a studio job BUT gets thrown because of their lack of experience in following a conductor. To be able to follow a conductor is an absolute must for a studio player (especially in Movie and TV work). There are good and bad conductors in the Studio business. Regardless of their capabilities you must be able to follow both. Below I will give different examples and remarks of a conductor.

CONDUCTOR: I will give you 4 in front.

What he means is he will count out 4 beats in front of the tune. Then the orchestra begins (or he might say 6 in front or 8 in front).

CONDUCTOR: I will give you a down beat.

The conductor lifts his baton and brings it down. When his baton is down, the orchestra starts playing. (Watch where his down beat on the baton is.) It will give you a clue on his conducting for the rest of the date. His down beat might be a chest high, belly high or whatever but this will more than likely be his pattern for the rest of the date.

CONDUCTOR: This cue is rubato.

Here is where you have to watch the conductor closely. Tempos might change constantly in a song and you have to be able to follow accordingly. Here is a brief summary of the type of arm movements a conductor will use in different time changes.

CONDUCTING IN FOUR (4)

Beat one (1)
    Conductor's baton hand is brought down
Beat two (2)
    Conductor's baton hand turns to his left
Beat three (3)
    Conductor's baton hand turns to his right
Beat four (4)
    Conductor's baton hand turns upward and goes back to the top

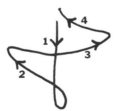

CONDUCTING IN THREE (3)

Beat one (1)
    Conductor's baton hand is brought down
Beat two (2)
    Conductor's baton hand turns to his right
Beat three (3)
    Conductor's baton hand turns upward and goes back to the top

CONDUCTING IN TWO (2)

Beat one (1)
    Conductor's baton hand is brought down

Beat two (2)
    Conductor's baton hand turns upward and goes back to the top

CONDUCTING IN FIVE (5)

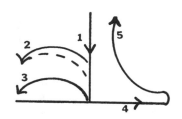

Beat one (1)
    Conductor's baton hand is brought down
Beats two (2) and three (3)
    Conductor's baton hand goes to his left twice
Beat four (4)
    Conductor's baton hand is brought to his right
Beat five (5)
    Conductor's baton hand turns upward and goes back to the top

CONDUCTING IN SIX (6)

Conductor generally conducts in three (3).
Two (2) bars in three (3) is equivalent to one (1) bar in six (6).

CONDUCTING IN SEVEN (7)

Beat one (1)
    Conductor's baton hand is brought down
Beat two (2), three (3), four (4), and five (5)
    Conductor's baton hand goes to the left four (4) times
Beat six (6)
    Conductor's baton hand brought to his right
Beat seven (7)
    Conductor's baton hand turns upward and goes back to the top

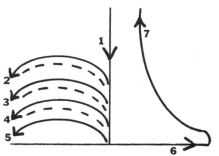

CONDUCTOR: I will cue you.

    This means you will not play until the conductor points his baton at you.

CONDUCTOR: We will be on click tracks.

    A click track is merely a time sounding device like a metronome. You will put head sets on and hear the beat coming from the head sets. This enables the orchestra to stay together regardless of how far the musicians are from each other. It also enables the conductor to get the exact timing he needs for the project.

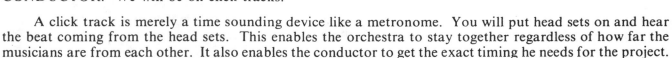

    A while back when guitar Pedal boards were just starting to show up in the studios, I was working with Dennis Budimir on a Bob Prinz date. Here was Dennis with his $3,000.00 pedal board and look at me with a wa-wa pedal and phaser attached to an old plywood board with rubber bands. On this date the leader, Bob Prinz, asked to hear a certain chord from me with phasing. I played the chord. Bob then asked Dennis for the same thing. After Dennis played the chord, the leader asked if Dennis could get the sound I was getting. Immediately laughter broke out in the orchestra. The leader didn't understand the laughing until later when we showed him my board versus Dennis'. I told Dennis he should have his board modified and try to re-create the sound of my $1.38 board. As usual we kidded about this for weeks in the studios.

STUDIO PLAYER—RECORDS

I think of the record business as divided in two (2) different categories.

CATEGORY 1:

The recording of groups such as Henry Mancini, Doc Severenson, singers such as Frank Sinatra, Tony Bennett, Vicky Carr and large orchestras usually fall into this category. The music is generally written out and creativity by a musician is minimal. The orchestra sizes vary from four (4) men to seventy-five (75) men. Most of the guitar work on these jobs are just rhythm type parts with an occasional stylized solo.

CATEGORY 2: (Records geared for the Top 40 Market)

This is the big part of the business for recording guitar players. Here, reading is not as important as creativity on a job. The record call will be started with just a rhythm section (1 or 2 guitar players, 1 or 2 piano players, Fender bass, drums, and 1 or 2 percussion players). Here they will start with a basic lead sheet and keep working until they are satisfied with a basic rhythm track. One of the last things to be put on the record will be the vocalist or the instrumental artist. I have done as many as six (6) or seven (7) three (3) hour sessions to get a basic rhythm track for an artist.

If a date is being recorded for a successful artist, a guitar player's career can skyrocket. These are the dates when guitar players become HOT names. Maybe a good guitar lick helped a record to become a hit. The next date another Producer might say, "Get me the guitar player with the HOT lick." Before you know it, everyone will want Mr. HOT licks on their record. Here is when he decides he is worth more money. He stays hot making a fortune doing record dates until Mr. Guitar Player with HOT licks No. 2 comes into the picture. In the meantime, Mr. Rhythm guitar player keeps playing rhythm behind all the HOT guys. No ego problems. He just plucks away and makes his taste.

Versatility is not as important in this phase of the business. If the producers need a mandolin player or whatever, the budget will warrant calling in a specialist.

Even though strong sight reading is not as important in this area of recording, there are always exceptions to this rule. You could be asked to do some rough reading because the guitar parts are all arranged for a specific purpose. (BE PREPARED.) The new method of direct to disc recording also creates a problem for a non-reader. It is virtually impossible to record in this situation without some kind of sight reading ability. (Direct to disc recording is a recording of one whole side of an album without stopping. If there are any mistakes on a recording, the whole side has to be re-recorded.)

The following music is an example of a lead sheet we work off of on a record date. The date starts with a rhythm section running over the chord changes. Then they start to invent an arrangement, changes of repeats, lengthening or shortening the tune, additions and deletions of chords, are all part of things that might happen. In the 1960's a little chord arrangement like this could have kept me busy for days if it was recorded for the likes of Phil Spector, the Beach Boys, Jan & Dean, etc. When the date is over, many times the chart is unrecognizable from the original run through. If you as a guitar player can add just one thing the leader likes, you could graduate to be his first call guitar player.

A Los Angeles record date player averages approximately $40.00 to $80.00 an hour depending on his status in the field (new player—$40.00, union scale; creator of hits—$80.00, double union scale; and super-star—whatever he can get). A record date is a minimum 3 hour call.

🍵 🍵 🍵 🍵 🍵 🍵 🍵 🍵 🍵 🍵 🍵 🍵 🍵 🍵 🍵 🍵 🍵

A few years ago I was working a date at A & M Records. On the second guitar was Mike Deasy. The new young producer in the booth decided to show off his wares. He asked me what guitar I was playing. I said acoustic. He said he would like to hear the part on gut string. I reached down like I was getting a gut string, but came up with the same old acoustic and started playing. He said he thought he liked that better. I smiled and asked if he would like to hear the part on 12 string. He said yes. I reached over and made him think I was getting a 12 string. Yes, you're right! I came back with the acoustic again. He said he really loved it on the 12 string. We made the take on what he thought was a 12 string. Mike shuddered at all the happenings . . .

🍵 🍵 🍵 🍵 🍵 🍵 🍵 🍵 🍵 🍵 🍵 🍵 🍵 🍵 🍵 🍵 🍵

"TONGUE AND CHEEK"

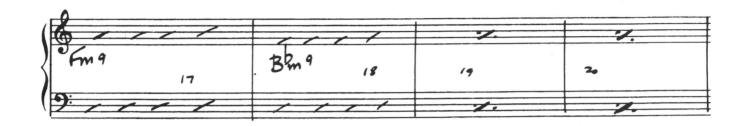

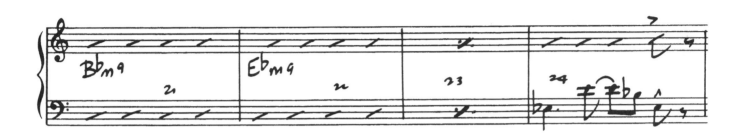

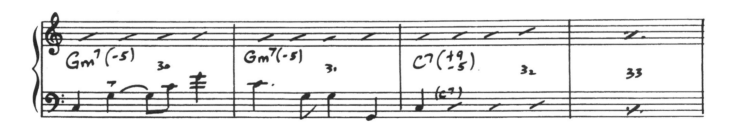

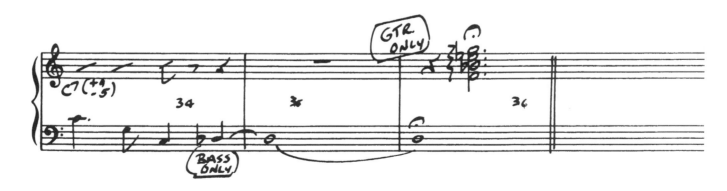

88

One day I got a call from a composer, Stan Worth, to do a cartoon series. On the job the music went back and forth from acoustic to electric guitar. Halfway thru the job I used my own discretion whether to play electric or acoustic on any given part. At the end of the day the producer seemed to like what we did. A few weeks later at a screening of the cartoon, the producer was horrified at what I played. It turned out the acoustic parts were for the pretty lady in the cartoon and the electric parts were for the villain. Being I played the parts with my own discretion, nothing fit what the producer had in mind for the picture. (My own creativity cost me work. I haven't worked for this producer since.)

STUDIO PLAYER—COMMERCIALS

Here is another facet of the music business where strong sight reading is not as necessary as creativity. Each cue is generally 30 - 60 seconds long, of which three (3) cues will be done in an hour. It might be an advertisement for a bank, new automobile, or a household product. There is usually a gimmick lyric with the orchestra playing a secondary role. Every once in a while a commercial will be called using a jazz player or a rock player for the background for a certain sound. If you cannot cut a 30 second cue, you really should be still at home practicing. Create a lick and you may get the next job.

EXAMPLE OF A COMMERCIAL

The following is an example of a commercial I did for Bob Bain (jingle arranger and also the guitarist on the Tonight Show). The other guitarist on the date was Larry Carlton, besides Bob and myself. The final result of the take was Larry, Bob and I playing finger picking licks behind the vocal.

The commercial wage is approximately $50.00 per hour. Being this is only an hour minimum, most of the money is made on re-uses. Every 13 weeks if a commercial is still on the air or on TV, a check is due to the musicians that worked on the original date. If you have a commercial that is still running after a couple of years, you can be sure it ended up a good paying job. (If the commercial was recorded in L.A.)

Original music by Bob Bain, 1974, Mulholland Music. Used by permission. All rights reserved.

Recently I was on a studio date that required me to play the oud. When I got the instrument out of the case, I was completely shocked: I couldn't tune any of the strings but the first. I decided to bring it to the studio anyway. When the leader came up to me for an example, I played him a few notes on the first string. He liked the sound, so we proceeded. I decided to use my gut-string tuned down a fourth to play all the oud parts, and whenever an oud part came up, I transposed my lines to make them fit. Fortunately, I did manage to get a sound fairly close to the oud. No one on the date seemed to have noticed.

STUDIO PLAYER —LIVE TV SHOWS

Live TV shows such as the Oscar Awards, Osmond show, Cher show, Perry Como, etc., are another part of the studio world. Here versatility and concentration are very important. Versatility shows up because many times there are guests on a show with a variety of styles. (i.e., country singers, rock singers, tap dancers, acrobatics) and a player has to know many styles to pull the job off. Concentration has to be maintained constantly because unlike a record date, you do not get another chance to do it over if you make a mistake. TOO LATE - the show is already on the air.

The money made on TV shows varies from show to show. I have made as high as $1500.00 on a show if it has a lot of music. Also a musician gets paid if they use any of the pre-recorded music for rehearsing even though the musicians are not present.

The music example shows a part that might easily be an opening of a TV show. You will notice the changes of tempo. A musician has to be able to follow a conductor to keep with the changes of tempo.

"TOMMY'S BALLERINA SHOW"

STUDIO PLAYER — TV FILM

Working on TV films such as Charlie's Angels, Rockford Files, Love Boat, Mash, Fantasy Island, etc., necessitates a strong background in sight-reading, versatility, and creativity. On a TV film show you might have up to 40 different sheets of music to finish in three (3) hours. Each piece could go from a three (3) second cue to a two and one-half (2½) minute cue. The Production Company does not have the time to put up with musicians scuffling on a part. Versatility and creativity spring to life because of the many plots of the TV shows. There might be a scene in the film of a Spanish dancer (enter Spanish guitar), young Rock band (enter electronic devices), a Dixieland marching band (enter banjo), an Italian love scene (enter a mandolin), or a Greek fishing boat (enter Bouzouki).

Being the music budget does not command getting a (mandolin, banjo, bouzouki) player for one little scene, you are expected to play the various instruments. Many of the jobs I have played these instruments on, have impressed the leader enough to call me back on other TV films.

A TV film player averages about $50 - $85 per hour depending on doubles. To record a TV film a player works from three (3) to eight (8) hours to finish the show.

🎵 🎵 🎵 🎵 🎵 🎵 🎵 🎵 🎵 🎵 🎵 🎵 🎵 🎵 🎵 🎵 🎵 🎵

I was working at Paramount Studios in Hollywood for a leader, Leith Stevens. Leith was from the older tough school of leaders. I was off one cue so I lied down on the couch near the scoring. I ended up falling fast asleep. It turned out a few minutes later during a soft passage of violins playing, a "god awful" snore was heard in the music. I woke up when I heard everyone laughing. The recording had my snore in as loud as the music playing. The musicians said this was one of the only times they ever saw Leith laugh in these type of circumstances. In the old days he would have had me thrown out of the studio.

🎵 🎵 🎵 🎵 🎵 🎵 🎵 🎵 🎵 🎵 🎵 🎵 🎵 🎵 🎵 🎵 🎵 🎵

ROCKFORD FILE — TV FILM

COMPOSERS - MIKE POST AND PETE CARPENTER

The following six (6) music examples were written by Mike Post and Pete Carpenter for the Rockford File TV film show. This music shows some of the demands made of a TV film player.

CUE 102 — Reading is very important. You can be the most creative player in the world, if you cannot read the notes, you are not ready for this type of show.

CUE 202 — Here is where creativity starts. A little fill on bars 9, 10, 11, and 12 sets a pattern of playing that you will probably use throughout the show. The description FUNKY fill tells you which type of fill is expected. Also notice the bending of notes in bars 1, 4, and 12. When I played this part, I bent the B flat note to C to get the C then I released it to get the B flat.

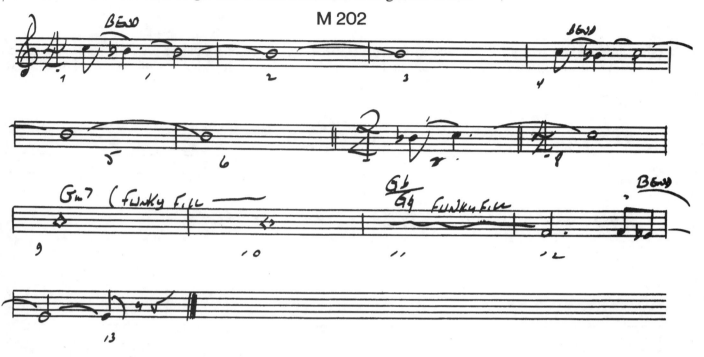

CUE 301 — Solo starts at bar 14 and goes to bar 20. Here is where you do your thing. If the leader likes what you did, more work will be coming your way.

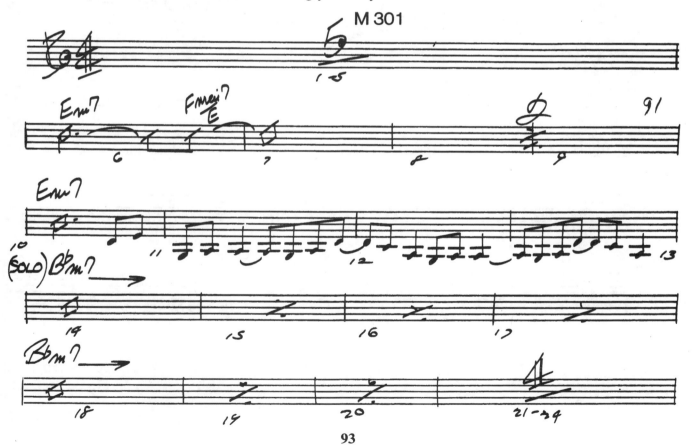

CUE 401 — You will notice it says Bi-Phase. On these types of jobs a guitar player is expected to own many of the different electronic devices (wah-wah pedal, fuzz pedal, phaser, volume pedal, or whatever is in vogue at the time).

CUES 501 & 601 — All right, guys — no solos but reading steps up in prominence again.

95

JIGSAW JOHN — TV FILM
COMPOSER — PETE RUGOLO

The following part was recorded at MGM with Pete Rugolo (composer of Family, Run for your Life, and many various TV shows) for the JIGSAW JOHN TV show. Again reading plays an important part of recording in TV film. Here is a part 117 bars long and we are required to play it without mistakes. (Many students that are pretty good readers never realize the two or three mistakes they made while playing a relatively simple part.) You will notice many changes of time signatures throughout. This can throw a new player. Get used to reading time signature changes.

You will also notice little syncopated figures throughout. In bar 78 tremolo back and forth between the E and D notes for three beats. Many times the picture dictates a shortening of the music written (Ex. bar 113 and 114 were taken out of the music). You would go directly from bar 112 to bar 115. At the top of the piece you will notice it says mystery sound. For this I added tremolo to the amplifier. You will notice on bar 109 and 110 it says cue. This means play if the leader asks you to play. If not, just count the rests. These types of parts are not for a novice reader. Imagine a show built around this type of guitar parts and the player called cannot read. Now it is destruction for everyone concerned, player, leader, contractor, and composer. Be sure you are ready when you are called for TV film.

96

97

MEDICAL CENTER — TV FILM
COMPOSER — GEORGE ROUMANIS

This music was recorded at MGM with George Roumanis (composer of many TV commercials and shows) for the MEDICAL CENTER TV show. Reading again is very important to a player. You will notice throughout the part George has many double stops and counterpoint (bars 16, 17, 18, 19 etc. and bars 32, 33, 78, 79). A player has to know the notes on the fingerboard, as George many times puts notes together completely different than the average composer. When working for a composer like George, you have to have complete concentration or you will get lost. After you work for many leaders, you will notice their music develops a pattern distinctive to their respective style. To work with George Roumanis you cannot be just an ordinary reader. If he stretches out, you need to be a real professional to get the job done.

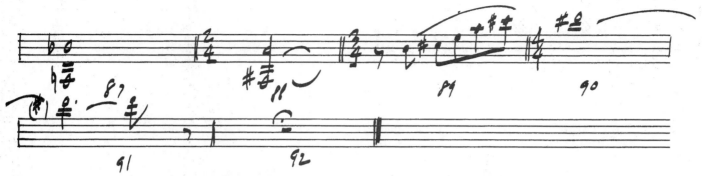

CONRACK — MOVIE
COMPOSER — JOHN WILLIAMS

Credit is given to Twentieth Century Fox Film Corporation for the following guitar part taken from the film *Conrack*. It was a Martin Ritt — Irving Ravetch production, produced by Martin Ritt and Harriet Frank, Jr. The film stars Jon Voight, Paul Winfield, Hume Cronyn.

Publishing credit for the music —   Music by John Williams, Fox Fanfare Music, Inc.

When I am called in to do a movie score, I am never sure what is expected of me until I arrive. It might be heavy sight reading, versatility (using miscellaneous instruments), or creativity (solos of different styles) one thing for sure is a must — COMPLETE CONCENTRATION. You might have a one (1) minute cue that they will finish in five (5) minutes or take two (2) hours on that same cue. It all depends on the status of the movie, the budget, or the leader.

I have done hundreds of movies but the following example was the piece of music that became No. 1 to me. To be able to pull this part off I needed heavy sight reading ability, concentration throughout, strong technique, ability to follow the conductor, and studio knowhow when to change a passage here and there. The composer on this date was John Williams, (Jaws, Star Wars, Superman, etc.) one of the top film composers in the world. After the job was finished, Lionel Newman, music director of Twentieth Century Fox, rewarded me with a bonus (virtually unheard of as a sideman).

Let me talk through the part and show my problems and how I corrected them:

Bar 10 — Earth feeling with a sense of freedom - I played the part with a folk feeling.

Bar 11 — I left out the middle G note to make the chord more playable.

Bar 18 — Instead of just sliding into the D note, I slide the whole chord to make it easier.

Bar 19 - 40 — I had to use complete concentration to know where the orchestra was to enable me to make my proper entrance.

Bar 41 - 48 — I started up high on the guitar neck and moved down to 1st position. This made all the double notes to come out clean.

Bar 52 — I played the D's and G's as open strings. I played the first two beats of notes on the 4th string to move along with the open D. I played the last two beats of the bar on the third string to follow along with the open G.

Bar 58 — Figure out a position that laid well with the run. (7th position)

Bar 72 — Solo espr — I played the solo very freely and tried to put a lot of feeling into it.

Bar 76 - 79 — The part was too hard for me technically. I asked and got permission to use just the top melody note for this passage.

Bar 82 - 91 — I heard the part was in unison with the harpsichord. I listened closely to be sure we sounded together.

Bar 97 — I changed three notes (you will notice the part) to make the run flow easily.

Bar 101 - 102 — Panic set in with this run trying to figure where I should play it. I settled by playing in bar one the low notes of the second, third, and fourth beat in position two. I went to fifth position to play the first two beats of bar 102. I went to position ten to play the last two beats of bar 102.

Bar 121 - 127 — I played all the notes either on the 1st or 2nd string all the way up the guitar (except for the open G in bar 25).

Bar 139 — On the closing solo I tried to play it as beautifully as possible with much feeling. The closing of a tune is fresh in the leader's mind. This helps for future work.

A movie player averages between $50.00 and $80.00 per hour. You might work three (3) hours on a movie or you might put in two or three 8-hour days. A couple of years ago I worked over sixty (60) hours on a movie before the music was finished.

103

104

LIFE SAVING DEVICES FOR THE PROFESSIONAL

When you have a tricky fingering that is repetitive, memorize the fingering you will use. This will help you in not getting lost after playing the figure many times over.

FAR OUT KEY SIGNATURES

The following example shows an unusual key signature. All it means is to sharp all F's and flat all E's.

USING OPEN STRINGS TO MOVE UP THE GUITAR NECK

In the following exercise, I would play in position two all of bar 1 and the first five notes in bar 2. I would then play the E as an open string to enable me to get to the last five notes in position 9 on time.

(To the traditional position player: I know I could have played it all in the 9th position but I avoid playing low notes in these high positions because of sound quality.)

If you are working with more than one guitar player, and a part comes up that the other player is more qualified to do, let him play it. This could save the embarrassment if you blow it, and they ask the next guy to play it.

Don't panic when a leader gives you bad advice. Some leaders will spend an hour on writing for guitar and they will act like they know it all. Don't try to look good by pointing out his mistakes. Believe me, he won't love you for it.

Don't let yourself get emotionally involved if the music you are playing does not agree with you. Treat the day as a necessary evil. There is music and there is a music business. It is not too often they will overlap. Get your fill of music outside of your work.

When I play parts that go from 4/4 time to 7/8 time, I use my pick hand to help me get into the new time. I always leave the previous time signature with an up pick leading to the next time feel. (Notice the pick markings on the example.)

When you have a difficult time reading a part, change it to a lower denomination. In the following example, mentally change the 32nd notes to 16th notes, 16th notes to 8th notes, and 8th notes to quarter notes. If you visualize it this way once. it will be much easier to play when you convert the notes back to normal.

106

On all the jobs be sure to be on time. You have to be pretty successful before you can become a "Prima-donna" (that's not me). If you are late for a job a couple of times, "Buddy, it's all over."

Don't be a nudge to a leader. Do not ask unnecessary questions. Sit there. Act and play like an expert. Forget the child-like ways of asking what I call good attitude questions. Don't show off your insecurities.

If you move to a big town to become a studio player, an absolute "must" is to join a phone call service. Don't try to save pennies and look for price. Get the exchange that the musicians use. It will definitely pay off in the long run.

After you have done a few dates, get a cartage service to deliver your equipment. The delivery cost is paid by the company you are working for. It makes you look more professional. If a leader says he can't afford the extra cost on a certain job, fine, bring your own instruments. This is doing him a favor.

Remember: No one knows beforehand where the 'Big Break' will come from. Treat every job as a big one. The young piano player might be the "Chick Corea" of the future. Don't make waves.

If someone asks you to play something you don't know, don't take chances. Ask for the music. Later on they won't remember you're asking for the music 'but' they will remember if you 'blow' it.

If you move to a music town, settle in a section where the musicians live. This enables you to rehearse or work and not have to drive an excess amount of miles. If you live too far away from what is happening, the tendency is to become lazy and you might miss that one opportunity that could spark your career. Stay in close at the beginning. When you are established, then you could move wherever you like. You will still get called.

GRACE NOTES IN READING

Whenever you see grace notes on a part, be sure you have the part learned first. Then add the grace notes. It is much easier to see the writer's intent.

Use your thumb if you have to play a part that utilizes a thumb technique. In the example below we use the thumb on the low F.

When we see examples of music written as below, it means bar your fingers across the strings and play the figure with no tonality.

In the violin section if a new player was called, he would never think of sitting in a concertmaster chair. In the guitar world the young kid comes in and is completely oblivious to this method of protocol. Unless the leader or contractor wants you to play lead or it is designated on the part, use a little touch of class. Let the senior member call the shots. Your turn will come soon enough.

Buy whatever new gadget is in. Don't be left needing something on a job you should have. Keep current.

Introduce yourself to the leader and contractor. Don't be a nudge, just introduce.

Collect and listen to many kinds of current and ethnic records: Italian, Greek, Russian, Chinese and Spanish, to get a feeling for that music. If you are ever called to play one of these styles, you will really come off as an expert.

Sometimes a chord can be played much prettier by using open strings. In the example below, play the low G on the 5th string open. Naturally, you have to lower the 5th string to G.

Sometimes a part is meant to be played on certain strings because it lies better. Try using different combinations of fingering in the example below and see what lies best for you.

Many times writers will take short cuts in writing 8th notes, 16th notes, and 32nd notes. The example shows some of their short cuts.

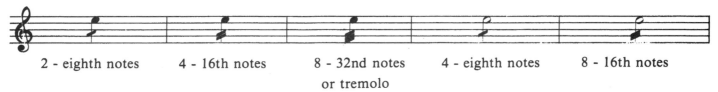

2 - eighth notes	4 - 16th notes	8 - 32nd notes	4 - eighth notes	8 - 16th notes
		or tremolo		

Play the instruments that the 'hot' players are playing when you are a newcomer. Leaders and producers do not trust a newcomer to set a trend. When you are one of the big 'boys' you can play a match box and the leaders will like it because it is played by Numero Uno.

Keep your eyes and ears open about opportunities. Years ago when Jim Hall was working with Chico Hamilton, rumors had it that Jim was being drafted. I rushed to where they were working. Jim asked me to sit in, I did, and Chico liked my playing. Even though Jim didn't go to the service, I started subbing for him when he couldn't work the job for Chico.

Recommend each other freely for work. The day might come when the tide will turn and someone you have helped will be there when you are in need.

When you have notes in groups of six or eight, sometimes you cannot see all the notes at first glance. If this happens, look at cominations of 3 & 3 for six notes or 4 & 4 for eight notes. For instance, in Bar -1- in the first grouping of six notes, think of it as D - E - F followed by G - A - B. After awhile the notes will start to register together.

When you have notes in groups of five or seven and you have trouble putting them in correct timing, divide the group. In the group of five, combine 3 & 2's. In the group of seven, combine 4 & 3's. For instance, in measure -1- of the example, think of the first four notes as C - D - E - F combined with G - A - B. After awhile you will see them as a unit and play them. Practice them over and over until the 7-note feeling feels comfortable. Do the same with the 5-note feeling.

There may be a time you will have to rest many bars. Try to listen and hear cues that will let you know where you are at. For instance: you have 44 bars rest until you play. You will notice the brass come in on bar 26 (check point 1). The woodwinds come in at bar 37 (check point 2). Now you only have to count 8 bars rest after the woodwinds make their entrance.

Whenever you see a part with chords written out, just play the part of the chord, then you can get it without making a mistake. Next time through, you will play more of the chord. More than likely by the time you make a take, the fingering of the chord will all be figured out and success will be yours.

If you make a mistake on a part, keep going. Don't lose your place in the music. You will have a chance to check it on the next run through.

If you find when a conductor gives a down beat and you are ahead of the other players, on the next run thru, play your note after the conductor goes to his next upbeat. Many of the instruments of an orchestra speak a little late. This has helped me to be in unison with them.

Have complete concentration when you are on the job. Keep your thoughts only on the music you are working with. If you are thinking about something else, an awkward passage will make you prone to mistakes. A few mistakes can lose you a job fast. Concentrate, concentrate, concentrate.

When you show up on a job, have all of your equipment handy. You never know when the leader might want to change the sound. Don't be lazy. It looks good to have a room full of guitars. It really looks like you know what's happening.

When you have a part that says 'solo', play it like a solo. Many players play a solo that sounds like it came from an instruction book. Think of the solo as a voice singing out. Change the time if you feel it. Remember, it's your solo. If this creates a problem with the leader, he will tell you. But more than likely he will like the solo that is you.

If there is more than one guitar player on the job, listen to each other and compliment one another. Don't try to outdo each other. Make it a beautiful blend. This also works if you are playing with other instruments. Keep your ears open and see if you are in unison with anyone in the orchestra. Sometimes we are so wrapped up in our own playing, we are oblivious to everything around us. The playback of the recording tells all.

8 VA (DOWN) READING

Sometimes a leader will ask you to play a part down an octave. Instead of telling him you don't have the notes on the guitar, be a HERO and lower your 6th string to the lowest note written on the part. In the example, you will tune your low E to a lower A. Now you have to remember to change any notes to be played on that string, to bring them up to the correct pitch. For instance: all the low D's will be played on the 6th string on the 5th fret. All the F's will be played on the 6th string, 8th fret.

READING "B♭" PARTS (TRUMPET, TENOR SAXOPHONE)

To read a B♭ part, just read it like it was a C part. Bring your hands down the guitar a whole step.

READING "Eb" PARTS (ALTO SAXOPHONE)

To read a Eb part, just read it like it was a C part. Bring your hands up the guitar one step and a half.

(To do the above transpositions, position playing is necessary. You cannot be thinking of notes since we are using the positions as transposition vehicles.)

If you are a player, keep in touch with the "outside" music world. My only regrets are I lost contact for over 20 years, but now - Baby, I'm Back.

Make all auditions. Every time I got an audition for TV, I didn't make it (too fat, too old, not just right). I nearly gave up on auditions. When I got called to audition for the Fernwood Tonight Show, I told them to forget it. They convinced me to come down and lo and behold, I got the job. I was sure glad because it ended up becoming one of my favorite jobs of all times. If you get called for an audition, do it.

The tendency if you are called for a job, 4th or 5th choice, is to be bugged. Don't let it get to you. Any negative reactions will show. (I know, I've been there.)

For longevity in the music business don't refuse other types of work. For instance, a hot record player might refuse to do TV shows and jingles while he's hot in records. After a few years when he's not quite in demand in records, what will he do if he has fluffed all the other parts of the business.

8 VA (UP) READING

I think of the guitar as having 12 positions. Then I think of the high positions as a small guitar with positions repeated 8 VA.

OLD WAY	NEW WAY
13th position	1st position (8 VA)
14th position	2nd position (8 VA)
15th position	3rd position (8 VA)
16th position	4th position (8 VA)
17th position	5th position (8 VA)
18th position	6th position (8 VA)
19th position	7th position (8 VA)

EXAMPLE:

The part below will be played 5th position (8 VA). Then read the part like it was in normal 5th position but up high on the neck (old way - 17th position).

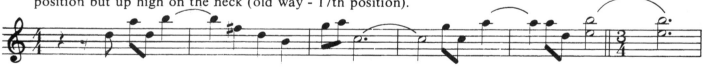

Always play with confidence. Don't let the leader feel insecure with you as a guitar player. He might not call you the next time.

If you can't play a certain passage without making a mistake, layout. Look it over. Then play it.

If a chart written is unplayable, change it until it is playable without drawing attention to the leader what you are doing. Don't be reminding the leader, who already knows he's not sure of himself when it comes to writing for guitar.

Where there are notes that are grouped together with legato markings, see if you can see a chord formed with the notes. Play the chord, letting the notes ring into each other.

Wherever you see groups of notes in harmonies and the part is moving a little too rapidly, pick out a few of the notes and just play the top notes. This will make the part sound cleaner. In the following example I have circled the groups where I would have left out the bottom note.

Thank the leader or contractor for the job when it's over. Enough said - go on your way.

Don't take a job from another guitar player because you work cheaper. He'll never forget it.

Don't lock yourself into any job if you want to be a studio player. If you are working a club and they won't let you off to do a studio type call, leave. Your future is being jeopardized. Even the biggest shows in the country, "Tonight Show, Merve Griffin, Dinah Shore", all the players are allowed to take off for another thing.

MUSIC INDEX

Numbers correspond to term definitions on page 113.

MUSIC INDEX

1. Treble clef-guitar is written in this clef.
2. accel - accelerando - increase speed gradually.
3. double bar - signifies end of music, phrases, or time signatures.
4. Adagio - very slow.
5. ad lib - improvise, fake it.
6. allegretto - fast, but not as fast as allegro.
7. allegro - fast.
8. andante - very slow.
9. andantino - slow but faster than andante.
10. animato - animated.
11. con spirito - with spirit.
12. crescendo - gradual volume increase.
13. diminuendo - gradual volume decrease (also known as decrescendo).
14. D.C. - da capo - back to beginning.
15. D.C. al fine - da capo al fine - go to beginning to "fine" (end) (stop at "fine" sign).
16. divisi - divide parts - occurs when two instruments are playing unison and composer wants them to take different parts at that point.
17. alla breve - cut time (with brevity).
18. dolce - sweetly.
19. expressio - expressive.
20. f - Forte - loud.
21. ff - Fortissimo - very loud.
22. ᴡᴡ - glissando - slide down from one note to next (the ones between the sign: ᴡᴡ).
23. grandioso - grandly.
24. glissando (ᴡᴡ) - slide up from note before sign to note after sign.
25. largetto - broadly.
26. largo - broadly, slower than largetto.
27. legato - smoothly - connected.
28. ⌒ a legato slur - play connected.
29. lento - slow.
30. mf - mezzo forte - moderately loud.
31. meno mosso - with less speed than before.
32. pp - pianissimo - very soft in volume.
33. p - piano - soft in volume (louder than pianissimo).
34. piu mosso - a little faster than before.
35. poco a poco - little by little.
36. presto - quickly.
37. prestissimo - very quickly.
38. rit. - ritardando - retard speed (go slower).
39. rubato - not in strict time (take liberties with your time interpretation).
40. a tempo - back to strict time.
41. tempo di marcia - march tempo.
42. tempo de valse - waltz tempo.
43. rall. - rallentando - gradually slower.
44. ⌢ - formata - placed over a note that is to be sustained longher than usual — conductor usually wants note held until he gives you cutoff signal.
45. vivace - lively, fast (very fast).
46. poco mosso - a steady pace slower than before.
47. tenuto - hold a little.
48. ten - tenuto.
49. 𝄋 - signo - sign - a reference point that is returned to in a piece because of importance, such as a chorus, It is returned to after seeing D.S. (Dal Signo) which means go back to the sign. (You'll see D.S. later on in this music.)
50. vib. - vibrato - wiggle finger of left hand to produce a slight pitch wavering.
51. 𝄢ᴡᴡ - trill - alternating rapidly between written note and note one whole step above.
52. : - dot - staccato - placed above notes that are to be played shortly and distinctly.
53. — - sustained notes but not running into one another like legato.

54. ∧ - forzando - accented with a bell-like attack and decay.
55. Sfz. - sforzando - accented with a bell-like attack and decay.
56. ♪ - grace note - play that note very fast with an on-the-beat stress. It immediately goes into note it is slurred to.
57. ⟨ - play chord almost as an arpeggio (use a slow down-stroke) called rapido.
58. simile - continue preceding notes in similar fashion (usually used to mark a reoccurring rhythmic pattern too costly to write out every measure).
59. > - accent - give notes full value with strong attack.
60. ⌒ -gliss - play note than a fast glissando down. Notes should not be defined in the glissando.
61. portamento - glide from note to note. If notes are not more than three whole steps apart, bending the same string such as in rock music might fit.
62. D.S. alcoda - Dal Signo al coda - go back to the sign ‰ and upon returning to the above mentioned D.S. al coda, go to the coda marking (the marking usually at the end of the music that looks like a gunsight ⊕
63. * - coda - ending of a piece of music. (See #62.)
64. ² 2 measure rest - (rest the number of measures designated at top of sign).
65. ⁄. repeat previous 2 measures (repeat the number of measures designated at top of sign).
66. ‖· ·‖ repeat marks - repeat measures between this sign and identical sign at end of a phrase.
67. ‖· ·‖ repeat marks - for end of repeated phrase.
68. cadenza - an improvised passage at end of music, usually a solo. Although traditionally an improvisation for piano in a classical concerto, in classical music today it is written out.
69. mp - mezzo piano - soft volume (louder than piano).

🎵 🎵 🎵 🎵 🎵 🎵 🎵 🎵 🎵 🎵 🎵 🎵 🎵 🎵 🎵 🎵 🎵 🎵

I was working at 20th Century Fox with Thom Rotella as the second guitarist. The leader was Jimmy Haskell, whom I've worked with on and off for 20 years (mostly off). At the end of one tune while the band was holding a chord, I broke into a jazz cadenza. After the take Jimmy looked at me and told me he didn't like it. I told him I am a creative player like all the young kids and when I feel something I just play it. He asked the engineer if they could dial this solo out. They said they could. On the next take I told Thom to do the same thing on the end. He said he would. On the ending I looked at Thom and he nodded his head and told me he didn't have the nerve to pull it off.

SCORE 1 for AGE . . .

🎵 🎵 🎵 🎵 🎵 🎵 🎵 🎵 🎵 🎵 🎵 🎵 🎵 🎵 🎵 🎵 🎵 🎵

TEDESCO'S CODA

All the previous exercises were put together with the hope you will use some of the reading techniques covered in the book. (Chord form reading, low reading, position reading, high reading, vertical reading, etc.) Reading can be important to a guitar player. It could be the edge over another creative player that cannot read music.

Lots of luck to you guitar players of the future. I hope to sit along side of you some day on some jobs and learn from you, whatever you brought from your world.

Tommy Tedesco

Tommy Tedesco

A Tribute from the Los Angeles Guitar Players

I have known Tommy Tedesco since 1955. When I got out of the Army, he really helped me and helped and helped me! Let me say right now, in print, that no one has helped players like this man has—hundreds, with never a thought about himself.

As far as Tommy's musical abilities and studio experience, they are certainly without peer: reading anything, no matter what clef or how high or low, or fast, playing any instruments. Also the man's uncanny sharpness or alertness of mind. Many times we would be playing a date, myself fresh, and Tommy after many studio hours the day before with a couple hours or less sleep and he'd always catch me in a mistake!

I hope I have briefly given a little different slant on Tommy. This book is of a type that has never been written before.

With all my respect and love,

Dennis Budimir

—Dennis Budimir

I don't know how I could ever repay Tommy Tedesco for the knowledge he has given me in studio guitar playing. When I first started playing record dates, I was fortunate enough to have worked with Tommy. Every time I approached something wrong musically, or asked the leaders a silly question, Tommy would straighten me out. Many times a young and inexperienced guitarist would make a mistake on a session, Tommy would take him off the hook and take the blame. Besides being an unselfish person, a beautiful human being with non-competitive vibes, he is the most-respected guitar player I have ever known.

—Jay Gradon

My association with Tommy Tedesco has been nothing short of an answer to a prayer. Being a studio guitar player was something I always dreamed about but never thought I would have a chance to prove myself. I accompanied him on several sessions just to see what was expected of a studio player. Right then, I was knocked down a couple of pegs. Tommy proceeded to show me all his little tricks and how he would handle himself in most playing situations.

One of Tommy's greatest attributes is his ability to adapt instantaneously to any style of playing. Tommy was instrumental in setting the standards for the modern studio guitar player. He is the Segovia or master of the studio and this book unlocks some of the secrets of his success.

—Joe Di Blasi

Among the L.A. studio guitarists, Tom Tedesco is the authority. He has set a standard of musicianship and professionalism that everyone in the music business can refer to, especially guitar players. Being one of the most successful studio musicians ever, Tom has "done it all," and knows just about all there is to know about the business.

Perhaps the best thing about Tom is his willingness to share his expertise with other musicians. It is not often that an expert in his field will take the time and effort to help others learn the ropes. Tom has, on many occasions, "set me straight" with what's going on, and other guitarists will agree—he's still number one!

—Tim May

LUNCH BOX ENTERTAINMENT
presents
A Film by Denny Tedesco

THE WRECKING! CREW

a documentary

Known within the industry as THE WRECKING CREW, these talented young studio Musicians played on virtually every top pop hit out of Los Angeles in the 1960s with their influential West coast sound.

FEATURING
APPEARANCES BY:

Al Casey

Bill Pitman

Bones Howe

Brian Wilson

Carol Kaye

Cher

Dick Clark

Don Randi

Earl Palmer

Gary Lewis

Glen Campbell

Hal Blaine

Herb Alpert

Jimmy Webb

Joe Osborn

Julius Wechter

Lou Adler

Lou McCreary

Micky Dolenz

Nancy Sinatra

Plas Johnson

Roger McGuinn

Snuff Garrett

Tommy Tedesco

"It was incredible! I felt just like I was sitting there with them at that table. It had everything I wanted to see and more that I didn't expect. Tommy's humor drew you in and the lifelong respect for each other was so evident. Thank you for making this film ecause it shows that these legendary musicians, who we listen to everyday, are anything but invisible!!!!!!"

Peter Frampton

"You'll gawk open-mouthed at the first hour of Denny Tedesco's documentary tribute to his father, guitarist Tommy Tedesco, and the astonishing group of Los Angeles studio musicians who were his friends, and so much more.

...This is a man's heartfelt tribute to an extraordinary father and his equally extraordinary friends and what they managed to accomplish in the world. If you have ever loved a record — any record — between 1960 and 1980, you've probably loved their work. And you'll find this movie deeply touching, very funny and a revelation."

Jeff Simon
BuffaloNews.com

"So many have tried to write about the west coast recording scene who really weren't on the inside of of studio work or who saw it from a quasi east-coast recording standpoint... Denny not only was on the inside, but he knew he had to carefully have all the angles noted and discussed by all of us studio musicians... that's why this film is so critical for the 'West Coast Story'... it's traight from the very musicians who experienced it."

Carol Kaye

DIRECTOR OF PHOTOGRAPHY RODNEY TAYLOR AND TRISH GOVONI   EDITED BY CLAIRE SCANLON   CO PRODUCERS JON LEONOUDAKIS, MITCHELL LINDEN AND CLAIRE SCANLON
PRODUCED BY DENNY TEDESCO AND SUZIE GREENE-TEDESCO   DIRECTED BY DENNY TEDESCO

WWW.WRECKINGCREW.TV